Nobody Chews An Oyster

SUSAN DOROTHY ('JESSIE') KEYSSECKER

Published in Australia by Sid Harta Publishers Pty Ltd,
ABN: 34 632 585 203
17 Coleman Parade, GLEN WAVERLEY VIC 3150 Australia
Telephone: +61 3 9560 9920, Facsimile: +61 3 9545 1742
E-mail: author@sidharta.com.au

First published in Australia 2020
This edition published 2020

Copyright © Susan Dorothy ('Jessie') Keyssecker 2020

Cover design, typesetting: WorkingType (www.workingtype.com.au)

The right of Susan Dorothy ('Jessie') Keyssecker to be identified as the Author of the Work has been asserted in accordance with the Copyright, Designs and Patents Act 1988.

The Author of this book accepts all responsibility for the contents and absolves any other person or persons involved in its production from any responsibility or liability where the contents are concerned.

All rights reserved. No part of this publication may be reproduced, stored in a retrieval system, or transmitted, in any form or by any means without the prior written permission of the publisher, nor be otherwise circulated in any form of binding or cover other than that in which it is published and without a similar condition being imposed on the subsequent purchaser.

Keyssecker, Susan Dorothy ('Jessie')
Nobody Chews an Oyster
ISBN: 978-1-925707-25-0
pp352

About the Author

Born in Brisbane in 1961, eldest of three children born to a police officer and a stay-at-home mum (they were called home makers back then). The author attended primary school at Serviceton and high school at Corinda. She studied Japanese from the age of twelve with the goal of teaching English in Japan. After working in the Queensland Outback, she taught English as part of her work over five years in Japan. She eventually returned to Brisbane and put herself through university as a mature-aged-student. Her career spanned a very diverse range of occupations including executive secretary, copy writer and office manager for a Japanese language newspaper, head waitress in a Japanese restaurant, and treatment scheduling clerk for cancer patients. Jessie is now retired and lives in Brisbane with a rescue cat named Thomas. Her hobbies, apart from writing, include pastel and watercolour painting.

To the love of my life, without whom
this book would never have been written.
To my Mum — an inspiration,
and my sister and brother, whom I love dearly
and to
the staff of VAGELIS Café,
who kept me caffeinated and focused.

If you enjoy this book, please feel free to share it
and to leave a review on
www.goodreads.com.au

*This is a memoir
and people's perceptions change with time.
All of the incidents in this book are
true to the best of my recollection
and without embellishment,
although some names have been changed;
either because I have forgotten, or
to protect both the innocent and the guilty!*

*'I don't care what the world knows about me ...
I just hope my mother never finds out.'*

– Anon. from a 1980s British cartoon,
not attributed by publisher, publisher not listed

Contents

Introduction	iii
LIFE IN THE SLOW LANE	3
Idyllic	5
On Strike	18
If the Barn Door Needs Painting	20
Shifting the Brick	22
Penny Picnics	26
School Days	30
My First Real Job	38
The Grandmothers	41
Scrag	51
Dad As a Young Man	53
Christmas Breakfast	55
Memories of Margarine	57
PLANET DOWNS	61
Planet Downs	63
Morning Glories	74
Curry for Breakfast	76
MYO (Make Your Own) Fun	80
CWA and Cricket	84

Mobile Disco	87
Outback Salute	90
The Grasshopper Plague	92
Percy	95
The Kill	97
Lessons Learned	99
Have Sister - Will Travel	105
Richard's Path	108

FROM THE GULF TO JAPAN	111
The Big Adventure	113
Kyoto and Nara	120
Shoe Cream and Cow Piss	125
Homeward Bound	129

GREGORY DOWNS	131
Gregory Downs	133
School Under the Stairs	138
Snake!	144
Visitors	146
The Gregory Races and Race Ball	148
Lawn Hill and Riversleigh Station Forays	167
The Business End of Gregory Downs	171
The Night Before	178
The One Mile	181
Irishman with a Machete	184
The Flat Tyre	188
All Toyotas Ain't Toyotas	191
Last Call	194

BRISBANE 197
    Ah, Soo Desu Ka? 199
    Singing at 'The Shoki' 209

A GAIJIN IN JAPAN 213
    WEC 214
    A Kid Called 'Shut Up' 226
    God Loves Carrots 229
    The Traffic Accident 231
    We Are Going to Cause You Trouble 233
    Another Lesson in Japanese Efficiency 235
    Nude Neighbours 237
    Church Bouncers 251
    What Doctors Can Do 253
    Living in Tennoji 257
    Lost Pup, Lost Child 259
    There Are No Kangaroos in Austria 264
    Reverse Culture Shock 266
    Bible College, Katoomba 270
    How to Find a Job 275
    David Jones Department Store 281
    University Days 286
    Japanese Plus 288
    The Cat Test 291
    QJCCI and AJSQ 300

ALONG THE WAY   **305**

    Last Hope   307
    Nobody Chews An Oyster   311
    A Scare   315
    The Firemen and the Cat   317
    Help, I Speak Japanese!   319
    Art For Everybody's Sake   321
    The Break In   328
    Another Crossroad   332

Book Club Questions   335

Introduction

My friends often tell me that they marvel at how upbeat I can be, often in the face of problems, illness, injury, unemployment, homelessness (briefly), or other obstacles. Sure, I used to believe that there was light at the end of the tunnel ... but with my luck, it would be an oncoming train. There have been periods in my life when I have been unable to drag myself out of bed to face the day because of Winston Churchill's 'Black Dog', depression.

It is not always possible to be cheerful in the face of adversity, looking troubles squarely in the eye, but I guess I am definitely a glass-half-full kind of person at heart. Trying to find the good in each situation becomes like hunting for the pineapple pieces in the topping of a Supreme pizza: the small, sweet bits amongst all the savoury. The first trick is to recognise them, the second is to enjoy them, and the third is to be grateful for those blessings to whomever you thank.

I think it is a good thing to develop the ability to be prepared to go with whatever life throws at you. Rather than bracing ourselves against what life hurls in our direction, we should roll with the waves as sailors do. Most of us spend our time struggling to change our circumstances, feeling as though we are stuck in the mire up to our necks, without necessarily asking what we can learn from each event or situation to take forward to use in the next adventure. For me, life has been a series of distinct episodes, with most of them building on whatever came before. We all make mistakes and I think that fact is comforting — we are all fundamentally the same. Life is not about the perfection of the destination — it's about the bumps, bruises, scratches, and the downhill freestyling without your hands on the handlebars, on the way. My favourite Japanese proverb sums it up perfectly:

Saru mo ki kara ochiru.

Even monkeys fall from trees.

Come with me on my imperfect journey through an imperfect and funny world.

LIFE IN THE SLOW LANE

Idyllic

Mum and Dad met at a café in Sydney where she was working as a waitress. They liked each other on sight and began to flirt. At the time, Mum had a boyfriend with a bright red sports car. However, she said to one of the other waitresses, 'See that man over there (indicating my father)? He's going to be my next boyfriend'. Dad persevered with his visits to the café, even though the coffee there gave him a bad case of itchy hives. Eventually they dated, and married on the 18th of April, 1959, in Sydney. My parents married young as was the norm in the late 1950s: Mum was just 17 and Dad was 20. Dad joined the Queensland Police Force, and they moved to an old house converted into flats on Dornoch Terrace, West End, Brisbane, ready to start a new life. They made friends with other young couples who were also tenants there. Sometimes, if there was something interesting on TV, one of the couples would run an extension cord to their TV and place it outside in the yard at the bottom of the back stairs. The couples would then seat themselves on the bleachers made by the stairs and all watch the program or game together. When my parents, starry-eyed with the optimism that comes from anticipating a whole new life, arrived in Brisbane, the City Hall dominated

Brisbane's CBD skyline (now it is all but invisible). They were married for about twenty years and then divorced.

I don't think my parents ever understood that, from our childish perspective and despite the fact that we subsisted on a young police officer's paltry income, they gave the three of us children an idyllic childhood. We lived in the country, in what was then the outskirts of Brisbane. Dad, Mum, my younger sister Sandi, younger brother Richard and I lived in a dilapidated and leaky old cottage on a property named 'Maryland Brae' at what was then Oxley South in Brisbane. It was a slice of rural delight. When we weren't at school, we were pretty much allowed the run of the property as long as we were home before tea time and kept out of the way of the property staff and the horses.

The Sullivans, who owned the property, bred and raced trotting horses. My father, Bruce, born and raised in country NSW and having worked as a jackaroo, trained horses to the harness of a trotting gig for the property owners and helped around the place when he wasn't doing his police duty. We lived there until I was about ten years old. My mother was a stay-at-home mum who did what housewives do, until we were old enough to be independent and for her to have an outside job. It would have been a lonely life with her only conversation being with small children. Luckily for her, there was another young mum living just across the paddock. Margie was married to one of the Sullivan boys, and became mum's best friend. I would often hear the two of them laughing together as we children played outside in the yard. Mum's and Margie's friendship has lasted all of their adult lives.

The cottage that we called home had only primitive amenities, unreliable indoor plumbing to the kitchen and bathroom and only cold water to the outside concrete laundry tubs. Hot water was generated by a old-fashioned chip heater for which Dad had to chop wood finely enough to catch quickly to heat the water for our baths, seldom more than a few centimetres deep. We had no indoor toilet, but a lopsided old, unpainted, grey, fibro dunny in the back yard. I hated going in there at night. We would try to go in twos and had to carry a *toad stick* and a torch. Some of the toads were the size of our crockery dinner plates. We had to wave the rough, improvised, wooden stick in the air to knock down any overhanging spider webs, and sweep it on the ground to knock any of the grotesquely fat toads out of the way. Once in there, we had to check under the splintery wooden seat for redback spiders. There was no electric light in the old dunny for many years. One of the jobs around the place that Dad hated the most was digging a hole in the mown lane beside the house for the contents of the toilet and burying the sewage whenever the tin bucket was full. I sometimes wonder why dads are given the worst jobs around the home (like putting out the garbage, burying the toilet contents, and punishing the children for infractions of the house rules), whether or not they were present when the misdemeanour occurred. Surely it is not just a matter of physical strength?

There were plenty of sturdy trees for three adventurous children to climb, including a gloriously fecund mulberry tree in the middle of Princess Thora's yard. We were admonished not to scare or interfere with the Sullivans' most highly-prized horse. In mulberry season, we would climb the tree with buckets and bowls and fill them for mum to make mulberry pies and mulberry jam. Of course, we would eat a large portion of the juicy, purplish-black mulberries as we picked, staining our fingers, mouths and clothes. We also loved the huge white cedar tree in the corner of the paddock immediately behind the house. The berries were poisonous, so we were told. We never tried, but took our parents' word. We were always dragging discarded rusty sheets of corrugated iron, cardboard and whatever else we could scrounge, up the tree for our makeshift treehouses. Usually, a strong wind from the west was all that was needed to knock them to the ground in an untidy heap. Then we'd simply begin again, like spiders patiently tend to do when their webs are damaged or destroyed.

We three children had a ready supply of snacks to hand at different times of the year: our yard had a banana tree, a flourishing macadamia nut tree, a mandarin, and the persimmon tree in the paddock behind the house. There were also passionfruit growing wild along the back fence. The persimmon tree standing alone in the middle of the same paddock was home to a solitary storm bird. We would hear its plaintive cry whenever we were a couple of days away from rain, and it was never wrong. Thus, it achieved its common name. I would like to pass on a caution regarding persimmons: never, ever attempt to eat an unripe one. It will leave fur in your mouth like a Persian cat turned inside out. Whatever was in season became our snacks which we were able to pick at will. The macadamia nuts that we carefully collected were so hard-shelled that they required either a brick or a hammer to crack them on the cement path at the front of the cottage. We were always in trouble for leaving sharp pieces of shell which penetrated the soft rubber of our thongs, unwary bare feet or polished black police boots, scattered along the rough edges of the path. Once tightly embedded, they required an idle letter opener or spare screwdriver to remove them. For the poor, unwary bare feet, there was little sympathy. One was simply handed a bowl of hot water, antiseptic, tweezers, and an admonition not to spill the water all over the back stairs.

As the eldest of three, I was able to earn some pocket money by mucking out stables, feeding the horses, and cleaning the horses' tack. I was also allowed to ride a pretty little grey pony called Tinkerbell, and later, another grey named Sammy. Nelly also belonged to the farm; she was so incredibly quiet ('quiet' here means 'having a quiet nature, very suitable for children'), so she was one of our perennial favourites. She would happily walk around with two or all three of us children bareback at the same time when we were quite small. Dad also kept his own retired police horse Joe in the stables alongside the trotting horses.

With Dad on Joe and me on Sammy, sometimes the two of us took long rides through the bush to places such as the back of Pullenvale which was then a tiny rural settlement. Dad, who spent a number of years in the Mounted Police stationed at Oxley, was keen to improve my riding skills and one day as we were riding together, said:

'You've never galloped Sammy, have you?'

'No, Dad.'

'Well it's about time you did.'

He reached over and gave Sammy a whack on his compact little rump. Sammy bolted and I hung on for grim death. Sammy propped suddenly and I sailed over his head into a patch of prickly pear. I stood up crying, but in his usual fashion, Dad said:

'Go on. You're all right. Get back on.'

That was typical of Dad's teaching methods. Back at home it took Mum a while with tweezers and antiseptic to remove the small cactus spines that had penetrated my skin.

There was a bad-tempered, half-wild, rotund cream pony that lived in the paddock beside the house. We would come home from school, change into 'yard' clothes and then go out to see Hossie. The pony was unnamed until we christened him as very small children who could not pronounce 'horsie'. We coaxed him over to the fence with proffered food and no difficulty as he was unfailingly and predictably greedy. One at a time we would leap fearlessly from the top of the wooden fence onto Hossie's back with no saddle or bridle, just winding our hands through his mane and gripping with our knees. We would compete to see who could stay on the longest. Hossie would bend his head around and try to nip us, or attempt to wipe us off on the fence, or would prop and make half-hearted attempts to buck us off. His disposition never improved in all the years he was there. He probably lived out his life within the confines of his paddock, reaching a ripe old age, untroubled by noisome children, once we had moved on.

The cottage was in a bad state. It was a ramshackle pre-war structure, cobbled together from wood and fibro-cement sheeting, with a small section of the laundry floor composed of metal from compressed car bodies (so I was told). With my head at the end of my bed, in the room I shared with my sister, I could look out through a wide crack in the unlined fibro wall into Mum's little garden, which consisted of a single flower bed, and held her pride and joy — large, deep-red dahlias. When rain threatened, we had to pull the end of my bed away from the wall. If we happened to be out when it rained, too bad; my bedding sometimes received a soaking.

Neither of our pets was an inside animal so they had to take their chances in the rain and usually found shelter in one of the sheds or under the low-set cottage. We had a 'bitza' this and a 'bitza' that, a black dog named Prince and a black cat named Tommy (an apt name for a tom cat). The latter adopted us one day from out of nowhere and would allow my little brother to drape him over his shoulders and walk around with him just like an elegant lady's fox fur stole. One day my brother decided to bath the cat by dunking him tail-first in a drum of stinking, liquid manure. Luckily for the cat it wasn't head-first! After that, Tommy really did need a bath which he didn't appreciate.

There was an old double bed festooned with a musty-smelling mosquito net on the enclosed verandah where my maternal grandmother would sleep when she visited. It was an open secret that Tommy used to sneak in sometimes at night and leap blindly onto the bed, slinking out again before sunrise. On more than one occasion he landed squarely on my grandmother, scaring the daylights out of them both, but not badly enough to deter him from doing it again.

One day Dad came home in the bright green Mini he had borrowed, and called us outside. He went to the boot and said, 'I've bought a new lawnmower.' We gathered around to see this marvellous machine, and when Dad opened the stiff boot lid, out jumped a fully-grown Merino ram! Billy actually became quite a good lawnmower, although because he was tied to a wooden stake in the middle of the yard, he tended to mow bright green circles. Later we acquired another, smaller, Merino sheep Bobby that had been kicked in the head by a horse, and proved to be of inferior intelligence to Billy. Billy had enough sense to be able to unwind himself from the stake if he'd done too many circuits, but Bobby would continue winding around and around the stake until he had no more room and was forced to his knees, bleating pitifully for someone to come and unwind him.

We were also adopted by a male brushtail possum, one of two common species of possum in Queensland, that lived in the ceiling during the day and came out to sit in the banana tree or on the laundry shed roof at night. Mum thought she sometimes heard someone or something grumbling and stomping around in the ceiling when she was doing the washing, but dismissed it as the vibrating of the metal section of the floor and the settling of the old cottage. We were first alerted to his presence by my sister one night when she was very small. The bathroom was too tiny to dress in, so we had to dress on the verandah, half surrounded by chicken-coop wire. The roof of the laundry lean-to shed abutted the roof of the rickety verandah but sat about 30 centimetres below it. One night while dressing, my sister looked up to find the possum staring back at her. She dashed into the kitchen yelling breathlessly, 'Mum, Mum, there's a big thing with big eyes looking at me!' I don't know who had the biggest fright; my sister or the possum. We went outside with a torch and found the possum by then sitting in the banana tree behind the bathroom. Mum returned to the kitchen to spread some honey on a piece of bread for us to offer the possum. To our delight, he crept lower and accepted the treat, though he was obviously very wary of us. It became a ritual, and the possum gradually became quite tame. Eventually, and judging from the possum to possum conversations we could hear during the evenings, he found a lady friend and moved away.

Snakes were a bit of an issue at the old house, and so were spiders; both of which Mum really hated. She had a run-in with a red-bellied black snake in the blacksmith shed one day while talking with Peter the blacksmith. It appeared to chase her out of the shed, but personally, I think they were just headed in the same direction. The grass around the house in the paddocks was quite high and was almost never slashed short, so it was a haven for snakes and other nasties. As children, we were warned again and again of what precautions to take to avoid snakes: make noise and use a stick to 'swish' the grass ahead, and thus we would give any snakes the opportunity to get away from us.

Mum had smoked all of her adult life, and even had a little cigarette-packet dispensing machine at home into which she had to insert coins in order to access the Peter Stuyvesant cigarettes. A man who worked for the dispensing machine company used to come to the house and refill the machine for her every so often. I never liked my parents smoking because of the horrible smell, but apparently, I tried to 'help' Mum when she needed her cigarettes by thoughtfully breaking the entire contents of a packet into halves — so she would have twice as many! I was only scolded rather than punished because my intentions had been good. Sometime later, when I was fully aware of the consequences of my actions, I put pinholes in each cigarette of another packet just below the filter so that she couldn't draw on them — I couldn't claim childish innocence for *that* one. Unfortunately, both of my parents were smokers and both contracted lung cancer. In the days when they began smoking, it was socially acceptable and no-one realised the dangers. Fifty years later, it caught up with them. My father passed away from the disease and my mother was diagnosed as having terminal, inoperable, metastasised cancer. Thankfully she has so far beaten it after two rounds of chemotherapy, ongoing immunotherapy, and an excellent oncologist.

 Christmases were especially fun. Mum would buy small items throughout the year, and instead of stockings, we had pillowcases full of gifts, none of which were expensive, but all were guaranteed to delight small children. Every Christmas morning, we were up early, rudely dragging our parents from the depths of sleep to the surface of wakefulness. We were eager to see what bounty Santa Claus had left us. Later in the year when we had played with and lost interest in some of our toys, Mum would hide them in her wardrobe and when we had forgotten about them, would produce them some rainy day; in effect giving us a second Christmas in the year. Recently, Mum gave me a letter I had written to Santa Claus at the age of six, which asked for some 'sope and perfume for Mummy and a tie for Daddy. May I also please have a toy mouse to skere my Mummy', proof of the family practical joking gene in action at an early age! I received a chemistry set, great for making rotten egg gas, a huge set of watercolour paints which fuelled my love of art, a crystal radio, a spirograph set, a toy ice-cream maker, a portable record player and a basic camera which kickstarted my love of photography. Dad made us a billycart from a wooden box and an old timber packing pallet, and a skipping rope for me which had the odd wooden ends of two of his disused, rusty tools. I had come last in the Grade 1 skipping race on school Sports Day because I had no idea how to skip. Apparently, I threw the loop of the rope forward, stepped over it and repeated it until I stoically crossed the finish line all the while being passed by competitors in other races. After that, I learned how to skip from some girls at school. That's the problem one has of being the eldest child — no other kids to show you how to skip, how to play hopscotch and hand to hand pattacake type games with their accompanying rhymes. I was completely reliant on my fellow students to show me 'the ropes' — pun intended.

Both of my parents had been brought up with corporal punishment for misdemeanours, and their parents had adhered to the biblical admonition that to 'spare the rod' was to 'spoil the child'. As little children, we received either a smack on the hand or a swat on the bum. If, after being told 'No' or 'Don't' once, we didn't comply, then we were smacked. I believe that you cannot reason with a very small child, and that such gentle persuasion as a light smack is very effective in gaining cooperation, however politically incorrect it may be now. We quickly learned right from wrong, especially when we were out in public. Mum was frequently commended, chiefly by older women, on how well-behaved we were. Little did they know that we had been threatened with an instant return home and smacked if we misbehaved while out in public with her.

As we grew older, misbehaviour was treated a little more forcefully — with the leather razor strop (used for sharpening knives and blades) that hung on the back of the kitchen door with its Harlequin's hat of thick layers of peeling paint. Thankfully, I was inclined to be a fairly good child, although I had my moments, I am sure. Most of the time it simply didn't occur to me to question a parent's instructions. Punishment such as a few stripes from the razor strop was Dad's domain mainly. I'm sure many children are still told, 'Just you wait until your father gets home!' That really wasn't fair as it cast Dad in the role of a fearsome tyrant.

Our childhood years there flew by, punctuated by both happy and sad memories. One thing that I remember vividly is that Mum had some great ideas when it came to fancy dress costumes for our annual school fancy dress nights. When I was in Grade 1, she dressed me as Little Bo Peep, cutting down and dyeing blue her ball dress to fit me. I had no front teeth but grinned anyway for the annual photograph. My sister wasn't old enough for school but accompanied me that night. She was transformed into Alice in Wonderland, with a blue gingham dress, a white pinafore and a white plastic rabbit with large blue eyes. Another year I wore a shift dress festooned with green cellophane and cardboard stars, as a Christmas tree. In later years I found I also had a knack for creating unusual and original fancy dress costumes. To one fancy dress night I went as a scarecrow (a broom handle, hessian bag, old overalls, four toy crows and a very, very old straw hat — I won the prize for the best costume); to another I went as a stove (complete with a whole chicken in the oven and pots simmering on the hotplates, one of which disguised my head. I won that one too). When a company for which I worked briefly held a 1960s-themed Christmas party, I made a long caftan, hired a long brown wig, made a ham sandwich with one bite missing from foam rubber and felt and carried a borrowed child's toy tambourine. As I walked through the entrance, 'California Dreamin' was playing on the hired jukebox and some people quickly and correctly deduced that I was Mama Cass from the popular '60s band 'The Mamas and the Papas'. Incidentally and contrary to common belief, Mama Cass did not choke to death on a ham sandwich.

On Strike

After we had moved to Doolandella, Mum went back to work when I was about thirteen. I have no doubt that she found it a struggle to work a normal work week, then come home to housework and cooking. She told each of us that we needed to pull our weight a bit more around the house as she could not cope with the entire workload. We had all made our beds and tidied our rooms (the latter, not consistently) from the age of six. Mum's admonitions went pretty well in one ear and out the other. Unless we were ordered to do something specifically, we did nothing extra without grizzling.

One day, Mum reached breaking point and had had enough. She announced to the family that from that moment on, she was on strike. The three of us kids and Dad thought she was joking and thought no more of it.

Suddenly, there was no fragrance of an evening meal cooked and ready on the table. Our school clothes and Dad's work clothes remained dirty and unironed. The bathroom was atrocious, the toilet foul, and no other cleaning was done around the house. Our school lunches remained unmade and we had to scramble to slap together some bread slices each morning, or go without. This lasted for about a week before an agreement was reached. We would now only be given pocket money upon the completion of appointed tasks. I took on some of the evening cooking which I enjoyed, and the ironing of Dad's seventeen or so work shirts each week, (I don't know of any other man who wore so many shirts in a single week — some of which came home with blood on them. Mum would just ask him if it was his or someone else's). Richard and Sandi were given some cleaning tasks, and the feeding of the pets. I also took on the weekly washing in Mum's trusty old Hoover twin-tub washing machine. It finally penetrated our slow minds that Mum did a tremendous amount of work at home just to keep things running. We gained a new appreciation for her efforts and did our best with our allotted chores. No one likes to be taken for granted, and maybe more working mothers should go on strike so that their families appreciate how much they do around the home.

If the Barn Door Needs Painting...

Our parents did their best to ensure that we did not grow up too quickly, and could enjoy our childhood. We were only allowed to watch certain programs on television, and were not allowed to go out with members of the opposite sex until we were deemed old enough, and even then, only under supervision. Fashion was not followed particularly closely — most of our clothes were homemade, hand-me-downs, or came from charity shops. I had the occasional new article of clothing as there was no-one to hand theirs down to me.

For Dad and Mum, having two teenage girls in the house must have been a steep learning curve since they had both been raised only with boys. My sister was a tomboy and then suddenly a fashionista. She wanted to have her ears pierced and wear makeup from her early high school years. The verdict on the ear piercing was a resounding, 'No, you are too young.' She went ahead and had them pierced anyway, and relied on her hair to cover them when she was at home. Of course, it was discovered, but by then it was too late. If either of us used makeup, it was always, 'Get that muck off your face. You are not going out looking like that'. As we neared our mid-teens, it was Dad who became quite philosophical about it. He would eventually sigh, shrug his shoulders and say, 'Well, if the barn door needs painting ...' My sister and I puzzled over his answer for a long time.

Shifting the Brick

When I was about seven, we were given a wonderful red kelpie pup Dusty that was the runt of his litter and that grew into a lively and intelligent playmate. Mum nursed him on her lap all the way back from Inverell, NSW. He'd not been away from his mother before and cried all the way to Brisbane, shredding the knitted nylon blouse my mother was wearing.

As a pup he was very greedy. Dad had made him a small kennel from a rough wooden Coca-Cola crate turned upside-down, with a doorway cut into it. I recall Dusty one day wolfing down his food as usual, but when he felt his stomach could hold no more, he stood up in his kennel, lifted it off the ground, and stuck one of his back legs sideways into the air so that his stomach had more room to expand. We all laughed because of his resemblance to a small, furry brown tortoise.

Dusty would become so excited when we came home from an outing that he would bark and run around and around the house for joy. Over the space of a few years, he kicked up the fine soil all the way around the house. When it rained, the well-worn track filled up like a moat and we had to place wooden boards over it from one side to the bottom of our steps in order to cross. Dad became really annoyed by the dog's behaviour and vowed to stop it. He went outside one night and put a brick in the middle of the Dusty's track. The next time Dusty ran around his path in the dark, we heard him galloping all the way until he hit the brick. We could hear him galloping along, and then, 'Arr arr arr arr' as he kicked it at full tilt. Being an intelligent animal, the next time he raced around the house, we actually heard the break in the sound of his running as he leaped over the brick. After that, it was an ongoing battle between the dog and my father: Dad would go down in the dark and shift the brick, and the dog would learn very quickly where the brick was and jump over it in his nocturnal circuits of the house.

Dusty used to await our return from school sitting at the very edge of our property at Doolandella, quivering with anticipation. My mother would stand at the top of the stairs and tease him by calling out our names one by one. Dusty's expression would be confused and a little shocked that although he was watching so intently, he had missed us ... and then he would realise that Mum had tricked him. She always maintained that when she did this, he would turn around, give her a filthy look and then ignore her.

Back in the good old days there was still such a thing as free home delivery. Dusty had all of the regular delivery men well-trained: the bakery man would save a stale cream bun for him; the milkman some fresh milk; and the Mr Whippy ice-cream man would save a broken cone and fill it with ice-cream for him when he lined up with the three of us children.

Our beloved Dusty succumbed to what we think may have been a poisoned bait, or possibly a snake bite; a sad day for all of us. He died a terrible death and left our lives as he had entered them: cradled in my mother's arms.

We later had other pets. My brother had a Blue Heeler-cross dog, Belle; my sister had a black and white shorthaired cat, Rastus, and I had an aqua-coloured budgerigar, Charlie (a birthday gift from my favourite uncle). Belle was kept on a lengthy chain so that she could still move around and have plenty of exercise. Every afternoon when we came home from school, we would let her off to run around the yard. One afternoon we were witness to a very funny incident which we had seen before, but had never given much consideration. When Belle was let loose, number one on her agenda was to do her business in the untouched bush at the side of our property. Number two on the agenda? 'Tree-the-Cat'. That poor cat was chased up a moderately tall eucalyptus tree in our yard every afternoon, and there he would stay, perched in the same small fork every day until Belle went back on the chain at dinner time. On the afternoon in question, we saw Belle straining at the chain and barking with unusual frenzy trying to reach the cat that was sauntering past just out of reach. Rastus casually strolled along past Belle's chain, and flicked his tail under Belle's nose, driving her crazy.

'That damned cat is doing that deliberately,' Richard said indignantly. 'I'll fix him.'

He went downstairs to fetch a couple of Dad's tools and some more chain. He lengthened Belle's chain by about 20cm. The next time the cat teased the dog, Belle, having extra length on her chain, clobbered Rastus right on the head and the astounded cat bolted.

I had trained my bird Charlie to fly to me when out of his cage. If I was lying on my bed reading, he would perch on the top of the book and with his beak clip little holes in the pages that looked exactly like the holes that bus conductors used to punch in passengers' paper bus tickets. Charlie loved music, so I often used to put records on my little portable record player for his enjoyment and mine. His absolute favourite was a piece called 'Chirpy Chirpy Cheep Cheep'. There was no way that the lyrics meant anything to him, but I guess he just liked the beat and music. He would actually dance to it, bobbing up and down on his perch and sometimes swing himself around the wooden dowel perch and up the other side. Unfortunately, he disliked men and would fly at my brother or father and screech loudly if they were in the room, so he was caged when either of them or any male visitors were around.

Penny Picnics

Sometimes, if Dad was home on a weekend, we would all pile into the old Holden and go on 'Penny Picnics'. I don't know where the idea came from, but we loved it. Mum would pack a picnic lunch basket and an old rug. The game involved driving until we came to a crossroad. Dad would drive and Mum would flip a coin and we would call heads for left or tails for right. There being three of us was convenient, because that way there was always a majority. Dad loved to tease my brother, who was perpetually frightened that we would lose our way and not be able to retrace our path to find home again. Once, out in the bush, Dad made each of us a 'duck whistle' with his ever-present pocketknife. This was done by partially splitting a short gum twig about one centimetre thick, and inserting a gum leaf, face down, which he trimmed to fit the twig. The result was a whistle that sounded just like a wild duck and set all three of us quacking. I don't know how Dad knew how to make such things, but I concluded that he had either learned from his father or brothers or friends, or innovated himself. Dad had a great store of knowledge of bushcraft and could make tables and stools from lengths of branches cut to fit with the sharp tomahawk he kept with his tools in the boot of the car.

Mum saved hard from the housekeeping money, and was able to pay for driving lessons in secret. She would walk across Hossie's paddock with its calf-deep dew-spangled grasses, and meet her instructor on Blunder Road. At the end of her lesson, he would take her home via Inala Shopping Centre; Mum would do the grocery shopping in lightning fast time, and load it into the car. She needed to keep her driving lessons secret as Dad could sometimes be cruel and belittle her efforts, even when she went to such extraordinary lengths to succeed. When she obtained her licence on her first attempt, she was so happy that she invited her instructor to dinner and her secret was out. It was a few more years before she would be able to buy a second-hand car of her own, — a little white Corona she dubbed 'Tuppence' — but it meant more freedom for her and also for us children.

Another example of Mum's money-saving ideas were our home haircuts. My sister and I had long hair: Sandi's was fine and blonde and mine was thick, dark and wavy. We needed the fringe cut every month or so and Mum's method of doing this involved placing a length of wide sticky tape across our foreheads, and cutting along the line with a pair of sharp dressmaking shears she kept for the purpose. We always had very straight, but occasionally lopsided fringes! My brother's hair was another story — Dad trimmed his hair with electric horse clippers borrowed from the stables. The girls in his class at school used to love to run their fingers through his crew cut, something that he alternately loved and hated.

There was even money to send my sister and me to Brownies and later to Girl Guides, and my brother to the local AFL football club. Mum even did a stint as an assistant Brownie leader, and as was the practice, chose an Aboriginal name: Bulooral, which meant 'night owl'. She and the leader, Joan Avery, became good friends. Joan's son Kevin was in my class at school, as were quite a few of the other Brownies in our pack, but there were still plenty of opportunities to make new friends.

Eventually, thanks to Mum's ingenuity and dedicated saving, Mum and Dad were able to buy a house and a three-acre allotment of virgin bushland. Problem was, the house was located at St Lucia, and the land some 20 kilometres apart. It was a two-bedroom, old cement stucco house, scheduled for removal or demolition: whichever came first. My parents' plan was to have it moved by semi-trailer to the partially prepared block of land in Doolandella. It came down to the wire. The demolition team was impatient and ready to move in, becoming antsy with waiting, and shuffling around in the heat, with sweat gathering on the chests and under the arms of their blue singlets. The semi had not arrived. Mum staged a sit-in with us inside what later became my brother's room. I remember that we were all crying. The texture of the old carpet and the musty odour of the place are inextricably tied to the terrifying feeling of being about to lose the only chance to have a house of our own.

She won, and when Dad arrived with the removal team, we were all very relieved. Roused by Mum, we stood out in the dewy paddock next to Blunder Road at about two o'clock the next morning, shivering in our pyjamas, dressing-gowns and sodden slippers, watching as the semi slowly went past up the low hill with our new old little house roped onto the tray. I think that was one of the most exciting things I have ever seen — our new life passing by us ready to be planted in a new garden, tended by the five souls who would call it 'home'.

As the only boy, my brother had his own room. My sister and I shared what was really the dining room, with its sliding glass doors and its varnished cedar wood picture rails. Much later, when I was in my mid-teens, we had an extension of two rooms added — the first time in our lives that my sister and I had had a room each. Mum was able to reclaim her beloved dining room, which she wallpapered, decorated and furnished with a great deal of care. I can remember Dad sitting at the dining room table with his old green Olivetti with its chipped paint and thick felt underlay, typing police reports with his index fingers, under orders not to scratch the varnish on the table.

One of my favourite photographs of Dad is of him studying for his sergeant's exams at the makeshift shelf/desk in the back yard of the old cottage. Another is of him on the back steps of the old cottage, smoking his pipe and wool-gathering, at peace with the world. Dad would always whistle when he was happy, and he had a great talent for it. Now, if I hear the British singer Roger Whitaker whistling one of the pieces he was renowned for, it conjures up images of my dad, in happier times.

School Days

I was and am a voracious and omnivorous reader and I clearly remember the day my whole family went to the local library, as usual, but where for the first time at the age of six, I was able to borrow my own books. The first book I borrowed for myself was Dick Bruna's 'The Apple'. Until then, Mum had chosen our books for us. That was a red-letter day for me. My whole family were keen readers. I am guilty of sometimes buying books that take my fancy before I buy food. An old maxim exhorts one to 'wear the old coat and buy the new book'. There are times when I have handed my purse to an accompanying friend before entering a bookstore as the only way to resist the temptation to spend anything there.

Because there are only 21 months between my younger brother and sister, they were like fraternal twins in some respects. As the eldest by a couple of years, I was the one mostly left to amuse myself, although we played together fairly well. I fear that as the eldest, I was probably very bossy with them.

One memorable day, on the 20th of July, 1969, when I was eight, all the students from my school were sent home early so that we could watch the astronaut Neil Armstrong take his first steps on the moon. Mum's best friend Margie had a colour television, so accompanied by Mum, we all trooped over to her home in the middle of the next paddock, and watched the historic drama unfold. From memory, it was televised in black and white anyway. My school did not have televisions for everyone to see the event.

In later years in school, I was a high-achieving student, but my brother and sister were less interested. I felt sorry for them when they ended up in the classes of teachers I had had in the past. The teachers made things worse by telling Sandi and Richard that they expected them to live up to my example. This was worse still in high school. Although I was a good student all through my school years, at one point I was very angry at my father. I had brought home a Japanese language exam paper with a score of 98%. This was the highest anyone in my grade had ever achieved. My father's only response was, 'What about the other two percent?' In hindsight, I would like to give him the benefit of the doubt and say that he was joking, but I didn't find having this achievement belittled the least bit funny. In fact, I was devastated.

I was very interested in just about everything as a child. A bug catcher kept me enthralled for hours at a time. We had a lot of milkweed growing near the house, and it was a great source of fat yellow, green and black striped caterpillars which we captured, fed and watched turn into chrysalises and then mature into beautiful monarch butterflies. We would feed the new butterflies with honey and water before they took flight for the first time in a brief journey of discovery of their world. Likewise, the mulberry tree supplied us with food for silk moths which we would watch go through the entire metamorphosis. This would be a rare thing for children to be able to do today. The only wildlife I abhorred back then were frogs, toads and grasshoppers. These dislikes have intensified and persisted into my adult life, with the addition of sharks. I would rather handle a spider or a snake and have done so with no qualms whatsoever.

There was no accessible kindergarten in the early days of my childhood, so when children in our area started Grade 1, that was the beginning of their school life. In my case, my mother taught me a lot before I went to school, so I was already a bit ahead when I began at primary school. I made friends with the most unlikely of my fellow students. In my grade two class, Troy always came to school without shoes, a terrible haircut and a deep squint. His family must have been too poor or uncaring to buy him shoes. He probably needed glasses as well. Troy was frequently bottom of the class and often wet himself. He was very wary of anyone in the class who showed kindness towards him. He would lash out and chase other students away. I guess I felt sorry for him. I always seemed to gravitate towards the new kids too, wanting to befriend them so that they didn't feel lonely.

I was never part of the 'popular kids' group, but was rather nerdy from my first years. In seventh grade, in an effort to make us recognise our self-worth in other ways, my teacher, Mr Hunting, held a Miss and Mr Personality contest. Everyone including me had expected that Pam Carson, the popular girl and leader of her own clique, would win. However, everyone (including me) was surprised when I won the title of Miss

Personality and it seemed that the other kids in the class saw me differently after that. It also meant for me that striving to break into the popular kids' group was no longer something to which I aspired.

The leap from primary school to high school was a scary prospect, because I didn't know any high school kids and it was all unknown territory for me. There was a choice of three high schools: Inala State High School and Richlands State High School in our immediate area, and Corinda State High School further away but still considered at that time to be local. I had it in my mind that I wanted to study Japanese and my parents had no objections, although there would be difficulties necessitating moving my brother and sister to Corinda Primary School. I was warned of the difficulty of the language and was told that a four in Japanese was the equivalent of a much higher mark in French or German. The two closest high schools only offered French and German. My interest in Japanese stemmed largely from watching the old series *The Samurai* in the afternoons after school on our old black and white TV. I had a crush on 'Shintaro', the main *samurai* character and I was captivated by Japanese writing and the lovely rhythm of the language. Most of that program was badly dubbed in English with only trickles of the original language allowed to filter through. With Japan being a major trading partner even back in the mid-seventies, at an early stage of the 'Bubble Economy', I thought it would be more practical to study Japanese than French or German. I had it all mapped out: after high school, I would go to Teachers' College or University and go to Japan to teach English, my favourite subject.

After taking me to meet with the headmasters from all three schools, I begged Mum to let me go to Corinda State High School, which, although the furthest away and which meant longer travel times, was one of the first in Queensland to offer Japanese. From the beginning, I had a feeling of privilege to be attending that school. The school was innovative in other ways, too. It had a farm and taught Agricultural Science, and ramps everywhere so that some of the kids from the local Montrose Home for Crippled Children could attend regular classes. I have always made friends easily, even though I can be shy and introverted at times until I get to know people. None of my primary school friends has kept in touch, but six of my high school friends still do, forty years on.

In Grade 8, one of my favourite subjects was Art with Mrs Autenzio. As an adjunct to helping us remember her name, she would count from five to ten in this way: 'Five-zio, six-zio, seven-zio, eight-zio, nine-zio, or tenzio'. My only previous exposure to art had been the little bits we did in primary school, and the odd project or two that I worked on at home. I loved making things, and something that gave me the most pleasure was the merry-go-round I had made from cotton reels, cardboard and cotton thread. The gift of watercolour paints absorbed me for hours and the discovery that colours had exotic names like Ivory Black, Rose Madder and Van Dyke Brown, rolling off the tongue like intriguing new tastes, was a revelation. I guess this was the beginning of an artistic bent that grew over the years. I have tried many different types of artistic expression, but love pastel painting and watercolour painting the best.

My parents didn't want me taking art classes in Grade 9 and beyond because they considered it to be frivolous and believed I should pursue more serious subjects. I loved English, Japanese and Biology especially, never understood Economics, just coped with Mathematics and enjoyed History and Geography — virtually everything except sport. I was not built for sport. I did try, though, and pursued cross-country running (which I found I did enjoy and was good at), badminton, gymnastics and ballroom dancing. I damaged my right knee playing netball, and more or less stopped playing sport when I could dodge it. First one knee and then the other were to prove the bane of my existence for years to come.

Music classes in Grade 8 were something I dreaded — I couldn't read music and couldn't seem to pick it up. I think my grade at the end of year was a mere 'pass', or maybe even a 'fail'. My classmate Carla asked me if I would join the Queensland Music Makers Choir with her. They were desperate for altos as they only had six in a choir of 60 high school children's voices. The children came from many schools across Brisbane. I asked my mother and she agreed to let me join. For the ensuing five years, I pretended I could read music. Luckily, I have an excellent ear and memory for music and the ruse was never discovered; sometimes I think the conductor had her suspicions, though. Mrs Christiansen would stop the pianist, her adult daughter Wendy, point her finger at us and search out any of the students who had hit a wrong note. I found that I could memorise large chunks of music at a time thus escaping detection for yet another practice session. We travelled as far afield as Grafton and

Rockhampton to compete in Eisteddfods. We won many times and only really had one serious rival choir. When I left the choir at the mandatory 17 years of age, I confessed to Mrs Christiansen that I couldn't read music. She snorted and said that she had had her suspicions even though she had never caught me out.

When Miss McKeon, my Grade 8 music teacher came to the school for a visit when we were in Grade 9, I excitedly told her that not only was I in a State choir, but I was also playing guitar. She looked at me in disbelief and said, 'You? Unbelievable, but good on you.'

I became involved with an interdenominational Christian Youth Group which met once a week on our high school campus and gave me somewhere to play my guitar. I met great people — trustworthy, caring and devoted. Somehow my goals changed and I decided I still wanted to go to Japan to teach English, but as an outreach tool, not for my own gain. I look back now, and see that at the time, I really did believe the doctrines they championed. Mum and Dad were having problems in their marriage, and it seemed I had an outlet for my teenage angst. I had an explosive temper and the beginnings of an on/off battle with deep depression.

I had my heart set on going to Queensland University after my high school graduation, but my parents decided in the end not to let me go. I think that the main reason was financial. However, both of my parents worked from the time they finished Grade 10 and perhaps they didn't see the need for further education. Gran had campaigned on my behalf to be allowed to continue my education to Grade 12. Unfortunately, her 'You've had your chance, now give your daughter hers', didn't work. Times had changed since my parents' teenage years and it was becoming difficult to get anywhere in life without a Senior Certificate and a tertiary qualification.

During school holidays when I was 16 and 17, I worked in the factory of Huttons' Meatworks at Oxley, netting $63 per week. Mum worked in the office as Receptionist, so it was easier for me to get a job there. I cleaned cans in the Cannery, packed sausages in the Sausage House until I couldn't count past ten, and bagged hams in Smallgoods — some of the most mind-numbing work I have ever done. To try to alleviate the boredom, I would sing to myself every song I knew. Nothing could be heard by other people as the machinery noises were almost deafening. I was very sure that I did not want to work in a factory when I left school, but having some significant money of my own for the first time was wonderful.

My First Real Job

After I finished high school, I hit the footpaths in the centre of Brisbane to try to find a job. I never made it beyond the third door I tried. I was offered a position at Barry and Roberts' Department Store, Queen Street, in the Handcraft and Haberdashery Department. As I had been undertaking crochet projects for cash for some time, it seemed a good fit. I was inconsolable when I lost my job six months later when my eighteenth birthday came around. My wages were to increase by law, and it was the company's policy to only employ the cheapest and the youngest. The HR Manager was gruff and intimidating, and told me 'not to take it personally' and he seemed surprised that I was so upset.

A few years earlier, we moved to the house at Doolandella which was separated by bushland and a creek from Inala. Because I had to catch a bus from Inala to connect with the train from Oxley, and I found that I was having to leave practically at daybreak for work and wasn't returning until sunset or later, I felt I needed to move closer to work. Besides, I was nervous about walking through the bush in near darkness by myself, especially since on one occasion I was attacked by a full-grown German Shepherd on the way home.

I was making $83 per week, and after board, transport ate up half of my remaining income.

There was a lady I knew who lived in Chelmer, which was about halfway between where we were living and the city centre where I was working. She had a boarding house for young women. I tried to broach the subject with Mum but she just told me not to be stupid. Dad was either at work or at the pub, Mum was about to go out for the evening.

'Mum, I won't be here when you get home. Here's the address to I am moving to,' I blurted one night, thrusting a rumpled scrap of paper at her. She left angrily for the evening, and I had to tell my brother and sister what I was doing. They both started crying and did not want to be left alone in the midst of our parents' deteriorating relationship. I was torn between staying and going. I knew that if I didn't move closer to work, the money I was making each week would not amount to anything substantial. A boy up the road from where we lived had been trying to persuade me to go out with him. I called him and said that if he would pick me up and help me move, then yes I would go out with him. I felt terrible for using him in that way, but he *had* said that if I needed to go anywhere, he would take me. I couldn't figure out how else to get to where I needed to be, other than to take him up on his offer. I packed two medium sized cases and a small cloth shoulder bag, and left everything else behind. My first steps on the road to adulthood.

The other girls in the house were also Christians and we all went to the same church. Sometimes I would be overcome by niggling doubt, and unanswered questions. I was told, 'You have to take it on faith.' Eventually, I felt I needed some freedom from all the household rules, and that was when I moved to Lima Street, Auchenflower, to a place of my own. I was also still seeing David at the time. He and I had been in the same classes in high school most of the way through and often saw each other in the year following our graduation. He was intelligent, articulate, and passionately interested in everything. We used to go hiking together, ice-skating (I still can't), diving, and we played heated games of Scrabble over long, interesting conversations. He was one of those rare individuals who knew something about everything — not cocky or arrogant; just with a fund of interesting anecdotes about many things.

After one long and fantastic day — hiking from the early hours of the morning through the early damp fog up near Lamington National Park, diving off Manly beach, then back to my place for a scratch dinner and Scrabble until the early hours of the next morning, David smiled wryly and asked if he should leave by the door or by the window. My window was ten metres from the ground, so it wasn't an option. We were more concerned with the nosy old lady in one of the front flats who felt compelled to comment on any visitors to my flat. Things between us had begun to change and I started seeing him as more than a friend. He didn't feel as strongly as I did. Neither of us was ready for that, so he simply stopped coming around. I grieved for him as though I had lost an essential part of myself. Over the years I made sporadic attempts to locate him, and never could. I felt a sense of loss whenever I thought of him, which was often. That was 1979: the year I headed bush.

The Grandmothers

As I was the first grandchild on either side of the family, I was named for both of my grandmothers. Mum's mum was Dorothy Levina and Dad's mum was Ivy Susan Maude. All in all, I think I got the best of a bad lot. I could have been 'Maude Levina', so 'Susan Dorothy' didn't seem so bad. 'Susan' was in fact a family name on my father's side which has been passed down through four generations, a fact which made me like the name for the first time ever. I have since discovered that 'Susan' also appears in my mother's family tree and 'Dorothy' appears in my father's. As a result the names I have belong to both family trees. In 1961, when I was born, 'Susan' was the most popular girls' name and 'Peter' was the most popular boys' name in Australia. One of my great-grandmothers, Arabella Augusta Susan Rooskov, glared down from my grandparents' lounge room wall and used to scare me when I was a small child. She was a big-boned, buxom woman with reddish hair (tinted in the old photograph), parted severely down the middle and drawn tightly back. She had a fierce, determined expression on her face.

There were four Susans in my class at my primary school, as well as a Sue-Ellen and a Suzanne. The rest of us were just plain 'Susan'. At the beginning of Grade 7, my teacher, Mr Hunting, said he would call each of the Susans by our surname or a nickname. He pointed at me and said, 'I'm not calling YOU by your surname. What's your nickname?'

'I don't really have one, Sir.' I was never going to tell him that my father called me 'Nugget'! I had heard it several times before but one of the boys piped up and said 'Jessica Kessica'. It was shortened to Jessie pretty quickly for obvious reasons, but stuck.

Through high school my nickname was there in the background but I was 'Susan' or occasionally 'Sue' to friends and family. In my first job after I left school, at Barry and Roberts, there was already a Susan working there, so 'Jessie' came into more frequent use around then. There was another reason for using 'Jessie' when I went to Japan; 'san' is an honorific ending put on to the end of a person's surname when addressing them. 'Su-san- san' was confusing for them. And 'su' can mean 'vinegar'. My surname made them baulk at the first syllable until I began writing it out in Japanese: ke-se-ka, and then it was easy. Together with Japanese friends, I chose characters that spelled out 'Ji-e-shi' which means 'song (or poem) of goodness and grace'. One of my friends had a very original, artistic freeform bamboo name stamp made for me by a well-known carver of bamboo stamps in Kyoto, and I still have and treasure it.

I think both of my grandmothers were very happy to have me named after them. My sister, two years younger than myself, was named Sandra Maree for my mother ('Dennise Sandra') and her godmother Maree Burke, the wife of one of my father's police colleagues. As the only boy, my brother was lumped with being named for great-grandfather, father and grandfather — Richard Bruce William.

We called my paternal grandparents 'Nanna and Pop', and maternal grandmother 'Gran'. In the six or so years prior to his death at 94, when we had the pleasure of getting to know our long-estranged maternal grandfather, he became 'Grandad'.

Gran was a go-getter. Married to my grandfather Glanfield very young, they produced my mother, then divorced, remarried a number of years later and then had my uncles Derek and Ian in succession, full brothers to my mother, who is older than her brothers by about six years. Gran and Grandad divorced again. Gran married twice more being respectively surnamed Wagner and Stone. John Wagner once took us out on a boat on which we slept overnight — a wonderful novelty, and all I can remember of him. Gran's home for most of my childhood was in Gladstone, and then later at Tannum Sands which back then was a sleepy, sparsely populated seaside holiday town. Her then husband George was noted for his home brewing, in the bathtub, and having the bottles explode due to too much sugar in the mix! We were allowed during some holidays to go and stay with Gran for a week just on our own without our siblings, and these were highlights of my childhood.

She took me to Hoy Parties, Cent Auctions and other strange and wonderfully arcane activities that I have not even heard of since my childhood. Hoy parties were like Bingo except the cards were printed with playing cards, and the cost of entry usually covered one playing card, afternoon or morning tea and the price of entry. Cent Auctions involved an entry fee which also included a lucky door prize ticket, and tickets to bid on items which might range from a one-day spa experience to Tupperware.

One holiday I suggested that she and I go ten-pin bowling. I didn't know she had never played it before. Instead of the run up, and bowl the ball from a standing position, she would run up to the line, drop into a lawn bowls stance and roll the ball from a crouched position. Apart from hitting the barrier with the ball and necessitating one of the mechanics to climb down behind the barrier and unjam it, you'd have thought she played it every day of the year! She nurtured my interest in art and on one holiday took me to visit the many art studios, galleries and artists' workshops between Gladstone and Tannum Sands.

Gran was a keen knitter and in the tropical heat of the coast she adopted a daily uniform of a pair of shorts, bare feet, and a strapless top of knitted cotton made on four needles (no seams), with elastic top and bottom. We told her they were popularly known as 'boob tubes' and she thought it was hilarious, although she thought she had invented them and so was a little crestfallen.

Another day, Gran decided to go through her photo collection while I was staying with her. There was a large moving carton about half-full of loose photographs and topped with a miscellany of leather-bound albums, brittle with age. Most of the single photos had no names or dates on the back, so while explaining each unlabelled one to me, she labelled the majority of them. It was fascinating because she would also explain the other people, the backgrounds and the occasions to me and unfortunately, most of that was not recorded. Thankfully, I assume most of the photographs went to Mum, and although I am probably the most interested in them of all the grandchildren, I have no one to pass them on to, so it would be best if Mum left them to my cousins and their families.

Gran's fingers were literally dripping with gold from the many rings she wore, usually several on each finger. One day, she and I were sitting in front of her dressing table at White Street, Gladstone, when she held out both of her hands to me displaying all of her rings at once. 'Well, which one do you want when I'm gone?' she asked matter-of-factly. 'I don't want any fights over them.' After protesting that she was being morbid, I chose a lovely dark-blue marquise sapphire flanked by four diamonds. I had always called it her 'butterfly' ring and would always ask to try it on, so naturally, that was the one I chose, and I wear it every day now. It is amazing how a personal piece of jewellery previously worn by a loved one can bring them to mind every time you catch sight of it. I think of my Gran daily and often have mental conversations with her, wishing I could ask her opinion or have debates with her.

Whenever Gran was in Brisbane, Gran, Mum, and the three of us children would try to get to the Shingle Inn Café in Edward Street in Brisbane City. It was dark inside, and very cleverly set out to look like the street between two rows of Tudor houses, minus the open gutters and chamber pot contents! We thought the arrangement of high-backed dark-stained wooden booths rather than table and chairs was wonderfully exotic. Some years ago, there was a fire in the Coles department store next door and a great deal of smoke damage in the Shingle Inn. The café was dismantled and the pieces numbered for cleaning, repair and re-assembly, but it never went back into the same location. After years in storage, the café was recently meticulously reassembled inside the newly refurbished Brisbane City Hall. So nostalgic for it are Brisbanites that one has to book a week ahead for a table. There are however, a few other Shingle Inns around Brisbane now, one in Queen Street and several at suburban shopping centres, but they lack the atmosphere of the original. Other inner-city cafes that have vanished from the streetscape since I was a girl are The York, The Renoir, Cubana, Kadoo's Bellybutton (24 hours) and Connections — all cafes popular in the Brisbane CBD in the 1970s and early 1980s.

Whereas Mum was the eldest in her family, Dad was the second eldest in his family of four brothers. Pop had been retired for some years when I first remember him, but had certainly had an interesting life. When he was first married, he was a butcher/slaughter man. He had been conscripted during World War II to work in the munitions factory in Lithgow, New South Wales, and had also worked as a 'powder monkey' during the construction of the rail lines from Sydney. Towards the end of his working life, he managed an ESSO fuel depot in Gulgong, NSW. My main memory of him is leaning forwards in his cane-bottomed chair, elbows on his knees beside the Aga, rolling his own cigarettes of Drum tobacco in his gnarled and work-worn hands.

Whereas Gran had a fiery temper to match her red hair, Nanna had a sweet and gentle disposition. She would occasionally lose her temper and be cross with the men for staying late at the pub, but I never heard her raise her voice or swear. One of the best memories of my Nanna was the Dolly Varden cake she made for my sixth birthday. It had a Barbie-type doll cut in half in the top, all covered in pink and green icing to make the top and skirt of the dress. I thought it was wonderful, and as she had had no daughters to practise on, I thought she had done a lovely job. The trouble was, the resident mice got most of it. I also baked my first batch of patty cakes in the wood stove that same year under Nanna's careful supervision.

I loved Nanna and Pop's house, especially in winter, when we tended to visit them the most. It was far colder in Gulgong, western NSW, than in Brisbane. There was the much anticipated *crackle* and *ssshpop* of tinder in the big old Aga in the kitchen and the grumpy sigh as the heavier logs in the lounge room fire shifted. It was my favourite place to read, slung sideways over the arms of an overstuffed black leather armchair in front of the lounge room fire. The leather was cracked from years of use and had a faint animal odour from the horsehair-stuffing visible through the many splits. My pages were illuminated by the flickering light of the fire. Much to my chagrin, a cousin I met with recently for the first time since we were both children said that her only memory of me was of me in that very position, sending her packing from the room with a single, silent finger pointing to the door.

We often made toast — thick slices cut from fresh bread

— over the glowing hot coals in the Aga using long forks, handmade by my Pop from fencing wire. They would be crisp on the outside and delightfully soft in the middle. Above the fireplace in the lounge room was a mantle clock that had the deep, reassuring *tock tock tock* of a slowly swinging brass pendulum. This is one thing I enjoyed back then, but I cannot bear the sound of a ticking clock in a room now. There are no clocks in my house, and I cannot even stand the sound of my wristwatch ticking at night on the bedside table — I find I have to leave it in another room or in a drawer when I retire. If I want to know the time, I prefer to check the digital display on my mobile phone.

Nanna and Pop were the only people I knew at that time who owned a donkey — not the animal but the wood heater for the bathwater, which Pop had to light every afternoon for hot water for everyone to bathe. It was a much larger version of our valiant little chip heater at home. I am very nostalgic for deep, claw-footed, enamelled baths, especially if they have the faint odour of the blue kerosene Nanna used to clean theirs.

Pop had an eternal struggle with marauding snails in his vegetable garden. The big, fat, slimy pests would have left shiny crisscrossing trails over the cement paths every night and every morning. Any visiting grandchildren were on snail patrol, we would each be given a plastic bag to fill with the pests we plucked from plants and the paths around the house. Most of them were then squashed and then thrown *holus bolus* into the rubbish. I couldn't stand to touch the horrid things, but would carefully pluck them one by one and drop them into my bag, holding their shells between thumb and forefinger, my nose wrinkled in disgust.

Nanna and Pop had an endlessly fascinating back yard, full of fruit and vegetables including a plum tree and an apricot tree which we kids frequently climbed. When the fruit hung fragrant, ripe and heavy from the laden boughs, we would scramble up the trees like nimble monkeys, picking the fruit for the pots. Nanna would wash the fruit, skin them individually by dipping them in boiling water for a few seconds or so, then plunging them into cold water. They were easy to skin then, and that was usually the job for whichever grandchildren were around, having washed our hands thoroughly after snail patrol! Next, they were stoned (the large seed removed from each piece of fruit), halved, then into the pot they went, with a large amount of sugar and some water. Then it was a matter of Nanna checking and stirring occasionally until the jam mixture reached a thickened state, ready for bottling. There was no recipe to follow, because Nanna knew ALL of her recipes by heart — jams, stews, cakes, puddings, roasts, etc.

Jam-making is a dying art, so whenever I chance upon homemade jams at a stall, market or fair, I browse through them to see if my favourites are there. As well as apricot jam, and plum jam, Nanna also made tomato jam, tomato and pineapple jam, and my ultimate favourite, tomato and passionfruit. It is sweet but tangy and is almost impossible to find now. Hot jam dripped onto unwary fingers really hurt. The burns had to be held under a running tap until the pain subsided. The jams were ladled into sterilised jars, allowed to cool a little, then a cellophane disk rubbed with an index finger dipped in vinegar applied to the jar's neck and fastened with a rubber band — again, a grandchild's job. As the jam cooled, the cellophane would be drawn down by the vacuum created, thus sealing the jar against mould, and pests, preserving it for several years. Some jam makers drip hot wax onto the surface of the jars full of jam, before screwing on a lid. Both are effective preserving methods.

Scrag

In the Gulgong backyard of Nanna and Pop's home stood a large, handmade cage housing the seventh member of their family: Scrag the galah. Galahs are a species of pink and grey parrot native mostly to the drier regions of Australia, particularly where there is grain or grassland of any kind. My father and his three brothers found the bird as children, and brought him home, thinking he had probably fallen from a nest somewhere. He lived to a ripe old age, even though as an old bird he had lost almost all of his feathers, leaving the wrinkled, naked pink skin underneath. Every time we visited, there would be Scrag pacing backwards and forwards on his branch-perch in the cage. We tried in vain to teach him new words, but he seemed to only remember the ones he learned as a young parrot. There was something that he did which I've never heard any other bird do: my grandfather had a terrible hacking smokers' cough, and the bird learned to mimic it so perfectly that it was impossible to tell if it was my grandfather up the back yard or the bird.

One freakish thing Scrag did which goes into the 'unsolved' basket was the fact that long after the four boys had grown and left home, he would start calling out the names of my dad or one of the uncles, and within a couple of days my grandmother would hear from the one whose name Scrag had been calling out, even though the contact was unexpected.

Scrag loved nothing better than to nip unwary fingers poked through the wire of his cage. He did like to have his head scratched, so at times there was a short truce between Scrag and visitors. As a younger bird, Scrag was allowed the run of the yard, only being locked up at night. However, my grandmother found that on washing day she *had* to lock him up, otherwise he would walk along the clotheslines and pull the wooden 'dolly' pegs off the washing and drop the freshly-laundered sheets onto the hard-packed earth below. She would then have to wash them all over again. Rather than being a pet, Scrag was more like a disliked, smelly aunt who came to stay every so often, with whom one had to be on their best and most tolerant behaviour.

Dad As a Young Man

The old wooden dunny in the backyard of Nanna and Pop's house had fallen into disuse with the advent of an indoor flushing model. Nanna had the dunny cleaned out, a new floor installed, the lopsided door rehinged, and used it as a small storage shed. With their 'Tex and Rocky' musical act in their late teens, Dad and one of his friends actually cut a record, for their act. Dad would be in a black fringed, white satin Country and Western shirt and his friend in the opposite. I never was able to hear the record because Nanna said it was 'somewhere in the dunny,' a less than salubrious resting place for the remnants of a budding career. Dad kept his guitar, a lovely semi-acoustic jazz guitar with inlays of mother of pearl along the fret board, which had been the second most expensive guitar in Palings music store in Sydney at the time he bought it. Later, at the age of twelve, when I decided to learn guitar, Dad's was the one I learned on, cutting my fingertips to ribbons on the light-gauge steel strings until my fingers toughened and calluses formed. On the advice of another musician, I would soak my fingertips in a saucer full of methylated spirits to toughen them up — a tip I have passed on to other musicians. In later years, when I had gone through a couple of my own, Dad passed the guitar on to one of my cousins, who apparently hocked it, thus removing it from family lore forever.

I don't think Dad was very musical as a child, and I believe he was self-taught on the guitar, learning from listening to his favourites such as Slim Dusty and Hank Williams. I have inherited his ability to play by ear, though now I mostly play mandolin. My uncle Darryl, however, learned to play the trumpet and it was still in what used to be his room. The only other impressive fact I remembered about that particular uncle was that he chipped a front tooth as a teenager — by biting his toenails. For a kid growing up, that was a very impressive fact to know about one of one's elders.

Dad worked as a jackaroo (stockman) in Outback New South Wales for a number of years until he decided to join the Queensland Police Force. He then married Mum and moved to Brisbane.

Christmas Breakfast

The trips to Gulgong and back by car with three tired and bored children in the back must have been quite a trial, and I know that at Nanna and Pop's it was no break for Mum — she worked twice as hard there together with her sisters-in-law while the men sat around drinking or disappearing to one of the local pubs.

I can recall a lot of bits and pieces of the many eight or nine hour car trips it took to get there. On one such occasion, it was June, very late at night, and a passing livestock transporter flicked up a loose stone which smashed our windscreen. We were about eighty kilometres outside Warwick near the Queensland-New South Wales border, and there was nowhere open for repairs. The temperature was freezing, and having frigid air blasting in through the ragged hole in the windscreen made us feel colder than ever. We limped into the sleeping town with gusts of cold air billowing around us. Mum improvised a windscreen repair of greasy cling film that had been wrapped around day-old chicken sandwiches, held in place with electrical tape from Dad's rusty old toolbox.

Another time, Christmas morning dawned hot and overcast with us nowhere near Gulgong. Dad, who was forever after teased about it, had missed the turnoff to his hometown, and we were now in a small town near Colla-bloody-enebri (as it became known in our family). Breakfast that Christmas morning was fruitcake, and cold coffee in disposable plastic cups that had held orange juice and still had the little pips floating in them, next to a concrete culvert by the side of the road. As governess on Gregory Downs, years later, I entered the northern Australia ABC radio's writing competition of the 'Weirdest Breakfast Ever' with that story and was given first prize — a copy of James Clavell's novel *Shogun*. Part of the prize was to have my story read over the radio. Veronica, my boss's wife and I were listening at the time and I was elated to have won — one of the first pieces of writing I had had published, apart from some poetry when I was younger.

Memories of Margarine

The high-set, dilapidated wooden house where I first lived on my own was divided into five flatettes and inhabited by eight people. There was a chain-smoking woman of indeterminate age in one front flat. She wore glasses with lenses as thick as the bottom of Coke bottles and listened to Charlie Pride cassettes for hours on end. A quiet, reclusive retired teacher lived in another. He was kind, and offered to lend me books from his small but thoughtfully chosen library. My flatette had a bed/lounge room, a tiny kitchenette and an even tinier dinette. The toilet and shower were down the hallway. My rent was the huge sum of $23 a week and I was so proud of my first flat and of the independence it promised, even though it was quite dark and dingy with carpeting so old that the pattern could no longer be distinguished.

A middle-aged Islander grandmother lived in one of the other flatettes on the opposite side of the hallway, together with her three small grandchildren. When she laughed, she would hide her mouth behind her hand and drop her head down. Her daughter had remarried and her new Caucasian husband didn't want the mixed-race children, so their grandmother was forced to take them in. The three children slept together in a double bed, and the grandmother slept on a camp bed at its foot. I used to give the children small treats, and to help out, I would braid the hair of the two little girls before school in the mornings.

One night the three children came banging on my door screaming, 'Sue! Sue! Gran's fallen over and she won't get up!' Fearing a heart attack, stroke, or worse, I ran the short distance with the children into their flat.

Their inert grandmother lay on the floor of the kitchenette jammed up beside the stove. She was unconscious and had vomited. I cleared her airway with my fingers, checked she was breathing and rolled her onto her side, grateful for the first-aid lessons I had had as a girl guide. I calmed the children, assured them that their gran would be okay, and ran to the house next door wondering if I was being too optimistic to ask if they would let me use their phone. They said no and closed the door in my face. The occupants of the next house along wouldn't let me in, but offered to call the ambulance for me. After giving them the details, I ran back to our flats and found all three children crying. I hugged them all, reassured them again and told them that the ambulance was coming.

When the ambulance arrived, I told the paramedics what had happened and what I had done to help. They praised me for my clear-headedness and quick thinking. They checked Mary over and soon had her sitting up. Instead of a heart attack or a stroke, it seemed she had been drinking vodka, slipped and hit her head on the stove and passed out. I was mortified and felt confused and more than a little stupid. I had a father who drank too much, but he smelled of beer.

Why hadn't I smelled the alcohol on her breath? That was when I learned from the paramedics that vodka has little or no smell.

Because she had hit her head, the ambulance men wanted to take Mary to hospital for observation. Conscious by this time, she slurred a little but refused. I offered to take the kids for the night, but explained to the paramedics that my flat was also very small and it could only be for one night. I slept on the floor and put all three kids in my lumpy old double bed to give Mary a break and time to get herself together. After that night, she would smile shyly but avoid me. I think she was very embarrassed by the entire incident.

The dishevelled man in the flat opposite mine kept very much to himself, and would only nod in response if I greeted him any time both of our doors happened to be open. I often wondered, but never learned anything about him, not even his name. He seemed very sad, solitary. Perhaps he had a mental illness or was a little slow.

One Saturday morning he was evicted by the rental agency's representative because he'd fallen behind in payments. He obviously had nowhere else to go, because he sat on the front steps slouched and dejected in the feeble winter sunshine. He was apparently there for some hours on the three wooden front steps of the house with his paltry belongings around him. Other denizens of the house came and went, stepping around him. The contents of his refrigerator sat on the ground at his feet, and one of the saddest memories I have is of his margarine pooling around the bottom of its cracked container on the ground among the weeds. That summed up his plight. At some point in the day while I was at work, he went away.

Two weeks later, we had a visit from the police to say that the former occupant had died, and they needed someone to come and identify his body as they had not been able to find any family, no matter how remote. Owen, the retired teacher, reluctantly volunteered because he at least knew some sketchy details about him, including the man's name. What a sad indictment to modern living when we don't really care for the neighbours around us.

A week or so after that, Del moved into his vacated flat and my future was soon to take a turn I had never imagined for myself. Del had been a governess at Tibooburra in the south-west corner of Queensland. Her stories were exciting and interesting. Following the split from my boyfriend at the time, and realising that I was desperate for a change, I knocked on her door on the spur of the moment and said, 'Governessing sounds great. How do I go about becoming a governess?'

PLANET DOWNS

Planet Downs

More than a thousand kilometres from home, I lay sprawled on my stomach on the broad and accommodating branch of a delicately leaved Samoan rain tree. I was silently watching a lone brolga, one of only two species of Australian stork, just metres away. I hardly dared breathe for fear of alerting the brolga to my presence. I hadn't been on Planet Downs cattle station for long, but I knew from reading that brolgas usually only behaved this way when trying to impress a prospective mate. The long, elegant grey neck dipped gracefully forward and then back, wings unfurled, high-stepping to some private music, scarlet patches on the sides of its head flashing. I looked for its mate. The dry waist-high ochre grass revealed no other bird. After watching the brolga for about ten minutes, he turned away and the gentle susurration of the tall, grass swallowed him. I couldn't decide whether the bird was practising to perfect its dance or, romantically, dancing for sheer joy. I was absolutely entranced. It seemed to me a magic perfectly suited to that magic hour. Our siesta was in the early afternoon when the comforting racket of the generator engine was silent, the men were at rest in the stifling heat, and the homestead dozed white-hot in the blistering afternoon sun.

Sharing with anyone what I had witnessed would have risked ridicule and disbelief and detracted from the sense of wonder I had felt. I could not have stood being told I must have been mistaken, that brolgas just didn't do that. Until now I have kept the experience carefully locked away in a seldom-opened mental filing cabinet full of my most precious memories. Sometimes miracles may only have a single witness.

Since the day after I had arrived at the age of 18, I had found that it was too hot to rest at this time on the iron bedstead in my room. Even though it was a highly-coveted corner room, with French doors opening onto two sides of the wide, screened verandah instead of windows, there was not even a whisper of breeze for relief. Instead, ignoring the fact of my advanced age, I shinnied up the tree in front of the house referred to as 'the second house' relaxed in the manner of a cheetah resting on a tree branch and settled down to read one of the books Mrs Dorrington had lent me. It was there that I was introduced to the delights of PG Wodehouse's Bertie Wooster and Jeeves the butler.

There were a couple of instances when I fell asleep in the tree and rolled off the branch, rudely awoken as I landed with a loud thud on the parched earth below. Twice I skinned my knees. Mrs Dorrington painted my knees with Gentian Violet to prevent infection and shook her head. 'How old are you?' she would ask.

Mrs Dorrington was a very large and formidable lady usually dressed in a sleeveless floral print dress. She wore glasses with such thick lenses that they made her eyes seem tiny, like I imagine those of a badger or some other burrowing animal to be. She was a retired teacher and loved reading, a habit which she encouraged wherever she saw a glimmer of interest in someone. Mrs Dorrington was known universally as 'Mrs D', and nobody could mistake her booming voice. As boss of the homestead, she was strict but very fair in her dealings with me and the others on the station and showed me nothing but kindness. She later wrote a reference for me in which she remarked that I was 'cheerful, with good manners and competent'.

Until two weeks prior to my arrival on Planet Downs, I had been working in a bistro in Indooroopilly Shopping Town in Brisbane, spending my lunchtimes munching on a sandwich as I stood unobtrusively watching a local portrait artist paint with pastels outside an art supply shop a few shops distance from the bistro. This was my second exposure to the amazing medium of soft pastels and influenced my love of them as a painting medium. I met that artist some twenty-five years later as a practising artist myself and was able to tell him what a strong influence he and his work had been on my own artistic choices in following years.

I scanned the 'Wanted' ads in the *Queensland Country Life* newspaper as Del had suggested, and found several 'governess wanted' advertisements. How to decide where to go? In a pragmatic moment, I asked myself which I preferred: mutton or beef. Mutton (no, never lamb — they all went to market) meant going south, beef meant going north. I chose beef and found myself caught up in a whirlwind of preparations, explanations, purchasing teaching books and books suited to Tina's age group.

After the interview, and the acceptance, I had a two-day crash course on teaching at the Distance Education Centre then based in West End. This was the only teacher training I ever received; apart from that I fly by the seat of my pants, gut instinct, and constantly striving to put myself in my students' shoes. There was a hastily convened party to farewell friends, who were mostly sure I'd be back in Brisbane in a week or so. I had two weeks to pack, move out of my flat, and fly to Townsville where I was to be met by the owner of the general store in Burketown in the Gulf of Carpentaria. Burketown was about 120 kilometres further north of Planet Downs. The owner of the General Store there had to pass Planet on the way home with a truckload of supplies for his store. His driving me to Planet Downs was a favour to Mr and Mrs Dorrington, for whom I was to work. I was to have travelled by train from Townsville to Mt Isa, but parts of the track were still under water from the tail end of the wet season. My student was to be Mr and Mrs Dorrington's nine-year-old Tina, the youngest of a brood of five by about eight years.

The journey was an interminable 26 hours, cramped in the middle of the bench seat of an old diesel truck bearing more rust than white paint. I had sat with my legs either side of the gear stick, a burly, tanned, Outback-type man on either side of me. We arrived at the Gregory Hotel just after dark the following evening. Heads turned and elbows dug sides as all the bar-flies sized up the new governess for Planet Downs. Unknown to me at the time, Planet Downs was a mere 15 kilometres further up the dirt road, but no one ever drove past the pub. It was the hub of the district; the place to go when you wanted to catch up on the latest gossip over a cold beer or rum. More than anything, I wanted the endless journey over, a shower, a chance to unfurl my kinked and knotted muscles and the blissful escape of sleep. My two fellow travellers were not beyond having yet another joke at my expense — they had been feeding me preposterous stories, lukewarm coffee and dried-up sandwiches over the past day and a half. They now told me we still had nearly 200 kilometres to go.

After twenty minutes of slaking our thirst and my being introduced to a maze of people whose names I could never hope to remember, we hit the road again. I settled into my now-familiar contortionist's position wrapped around the gear stick. Anticipating about another two and a half to three hours more of staring through the windscreen at the eerie apparitions of kangaroos, large birds and cattle that would suddenly rear up in front of us, I was willing us not to hit anything. Suddenly, fifteen minutes into the trip, we slowed and turned to the left along a narrow track which I assumed was a less-travelled section of the rough red-dirt road. Ian the driver, suddenly stopped and turned to me. 'Right, you can get out here,' he said huffily. I was bewildered and wondered what wrong I had committed. Seeing the baffled look on my face, both men burst out laughing, obviously having planned exactly this moment. Ian bumped me with his shoulder and smirked, 'Nah, we're here already.'

I was so tired I could barely stand. The wet season had just ended and the air was as thick as a heavy wadding quilt. Not only was it difficult to breathe the weighty air, but my limbs also moved as though I was attempting to walk through molasses. I met the family in a whirl of faces. I was dazed and more tired than I could ever remember. That first night, I was to sleep in a room in the 'Main House' with Tina. I remember seeing a pair of fireflies dancing languidly in the viscous air above me. I never saw fireflies there again so it remained a special welcome to the Gulf of Carpentaria.

When I was told the size of Planet Downs, the numbers were so huge that they proved beyond my imagination. Cattle stations in the Gulf of Carpentaria are so large that they are measured in so many hundred-square kilometres. What was then Planet Downs had been earlier split from Gregory Downs, from which the district derived its name, and earlier than that from the explorer for whom the river and area were named. Since the early years of the 20th century, Planet Downs had been a property in its own right, owned and run by the Dorrington family. With such vast distances to cover, it is little wonder that keeping boundary fences maintained is practically a full-time job on its own, and that there are men (and a few women) in that part of the world who identify their profession simply as 'fencer'. There is a saying in the Gulf, that the only time you eat your own beef is when you dine at your neighbour's, as cleanskin calves that wander over downed fence lines before the owners have a chance to brand and earmark or tag them, are fair game. A sort of unwritten 'finders, keepers'. This is why it is so important for the branding to be done while the calves are young.

The previous generation of Dorringtons introduced Droughtmaster cattle into their herds around the early 1950s, so they had a mixture of Droughtmaster and Zebu cattle. Both breeds have adapted supremely well to the dry conditions of the north-west, and can put on condition even in what seem to be poor environments. Having the perennial spring-fed Gregory River as the main water source, the cattle did well.

Some of the things I had to get used to quickly were the absence of electricity (only a diesel generator run two hours in the morning, and two hours in the evening), no telephone, no TV, no radio except for the ABC, and of course in those days, no computers. Our only means of communication with the outside world was the Flying Doctor's two-way radio powered by its own batteries housed in the station's office. This allowed us contact with the Flying Doctor for medical reasons, contact with people on neighbouring stations, and children with their classmates on School of the Air. Because it was so important, the station's generator had a shed of its own, and plenty of spare parts should it break down.

The 4 am and 5 am starts when it was still dark outside took some getting used to, and I was yawning until lunchtime at first. It seemed I was the only one on the station who needed an alarm clock and who almost hurled same across the room on a number of occasions! My role as governess there was varied. I was home-supervisor (as governesses came to be known), cleaner, assistant launderer, assistant cook and chook feeder and pig feeder. When it was mustering time, it was all-hands on horseback except for the two Mrs Dorringtons and the cook.

There was one little grey chicken that I hatched from an egg and imprinted upon myself so that it would see me as its mother. It would sit on my shoulder as I went about my tasks on the station. I called her Henny Penny. She was later taken by either a fox or goanna we thought. None of the rest of the chickens was named — I guess it makes it easier to kill and eat them when they don't have identities.

I was entirely responsible for Tina's education. Like other children in the Gulf, Tina was learning by Distance Education, and School of the Air. Children from all of the far-flung stations in the area encompassed by the Mt Isa Flying Doctor/School of the Air were grouped in classes, just as in a conventional school, and each class had a half hour a day on the two-way radio with their School of the Air teacher. It was their only opportunity to interact with children of their own age on a regular basis, and with a real teacher. The School of the Air classes were structured so that they meshed with the current lessons on Distance Education. The children were encouraged to call in answers to the teacher's questions.

Once a year, a teacher from Mt Isa on the PCAP (Priority Country Area Program) would come to visit the children station by station. This was an opportunity for the children to be assessed in their home school environment, and to see how well the home supervisors were teaching the children. Generally, they spent one night and day, then moved on to the next station.

Our PCAP teacher was Mark Murray. It is said that there are just six degrees of separation between one person and any other on the planet — I had worked with Mark's sister during school holiday work at Hutton's meat works in Brisbane, where she was the nurse for the company. I found that remarkable. What a small world! Mark was happy with the way Tina was learning and the way in which she was being taught. Sometimes it was a little scary teaching Tina, because often Mrs Dorrington would sit outside our little classroom and sew while I was teaching, unashamedly listening in on Tina's lessons. If Tina baulked and refused to do as I asked, Mrs Dorrington would thunder in through the door scaring us both and admonishing Tina, 'You were asked to do that. Do it now.'

Quite often, Outback children's teachers are their mothers. Usually, in that case, there would be a house cook, to take on the most important job around the station home. The cook's hours are very long, the work very hot, and in a lot of cases it can be a thankless job. In Planet's case, we had both home supervisor and cook, from Monday to Friday. On Saturday and Sunday, Mrs Dorrington and I shared the cooking just for the Main House and Second House residents. The ringers, both white and Indigenous, would make their own arrangements — usually meals at the pub across the river (a varied hotchpotch) or they would fix their own. If the men were out with the cattle, a tuckerbox would be sent out with them, containing damper, golden syrup, a large piece of corned beef, some cake, sugar, powdered milk and tea. The men worked very hard from sun up to sun down, and needed plenty of solid food to fuel them.

Planet's cook was a 'local' girl (from another station in the district, about an hour and a half's drive away) named Renee Porter. Tall and lanky, blonde Renee was my age and we became good friends and partners in crime.

After I had finished the dishes with Renee, set the table for lunch and attended to the day's washing with Mrs

Dorrington, school would begin. Classes were generally from 7 am until lunchtime, to beat the worst of the heat. The Distance Education material came by post on the mail plane every few weeks, and Tina's worksheets were posted back to her Distance Ed. teacher in Brisbane as they were completed. I tried to make Tina's lessons as interesting and as much fun as I could. I added arts and crafts, and physical education (a lot of which was horse riding) — Tina was able to teach me a few things! Even though I'd grown up around horses, a child born to it is more intuitive in many ways and Tina had been riding since she was about three years old — the shortest the stirrups could be hitched.

There were two pet dogs in the house yard, a sweet-natured golden Labrador named Brandy and a tan and white mongrel named Bailey. Not long after I arrived there, Bailey went missing. It was assumed that he either picked up a dingo bait, or was killed by a snake. People in our situation did not fret too much at the passing of a pet — animals are animals and people are people. Tina was the only one who really missed Bailey.

Dingo baits of low-grade beef chunks laced with 10-80 poison were dropped from a light aircraft through a chute in the door, outwards of a two kilometre radius from the homestead, so as not to contaminate water supplies (in our case, the Gregory River, and man-made dams and bore sites). Dingoes attacking and killing young calves was a constant problem. One difficulty with the dingo baits were that other animals such as wedge-tail eagles could also pick up the baits and die from ingesting the poisoned meat. They, in turn, could poison other carrion eaters such as crows and kites. I went dingo baiting with a couple of the men once. The plane flew very low over the areas chosen for the bait drops and would then suddenly swoop up higher to clear trees and scrub. Pilots in the Outback are a lot like the intrepid pilots in Papua New Guinea: if they come out alive, they are good pilots.

Morning Glories

After the washing up (for twelve or more people, it takes a while) for which Renee washed while I wiped, my next chore was to help Mrs Dorrington with the laundry for the station — sheets, towels and so on. The washing machine we had was an old-fashioned cylindrical one with a roller mangle at the top. The washing had to be done in the first two hours of the working day while the generator was running, with personal washing being done in the early evening. We had long clotheslines strung between poles rather than the ubiquitous Hills Hoists in urban backyards — crude but effective, and the same with which I'd grown up.

The temperature in the very early morning was pleasant, and I enjoyed the cooling breezes. However, the day heated up very quickly and we had to keep drinking water because dehydration was such a danger. The Main House at Planet had a large walk-in cold room, and this had a tap on the outside from which we could pour deliciously cool rain tank water. Tank water was for drinking, and river water was for everything else, pumped directly from the Gregory River. Using river water for clothes washing was interesting: no starch was ever needed because there was so much lime in the water that articles like jeans would stand up on their own after they had dried. The only other time we were allowed to use the precious rainwater from the tank was to wash our hair before a ball or local dance. The rest of the time our hair was stiff and unmanageable. I challenge any shampoo/conditioner manufacturer to invent a product that would solve that one!

One morning as we were washing, a very strange array of clouds passed quickly overhead, preceded by a great *whoosh* of wind. They were long, plump, cigar-shaped clouds ranging one after another in serried ranks. As each passed over, the temperature underneath would drop by about ten degrees. I had never seen such cloud formations and asked Mrs Dorrington what they were.

'They're called 'Morning Glories' and there are only two places in the world where you can see this weather phenomenon: the Gulf of Carpentaria and the Gulf of Mexico.'

The cigar or roll clouds, which stretched from one horizon to the other, continued to pass overhead for about twenty minutes, then, as suddenly as they had appeared, they were gone. They can be as long as 500 kilometres and as high as three kilometres. The cooler temperature left with them, of course. This is a unique phenomenon which arrives with spring. Morning Glories in the vicinity have been noted and written about since the area around Burketown to the north was settled more than a century ago. Scientists have theorised that they form when two opposing sea breezes meet above Cape York overnight, inversion and trade winds create a sort of shock wave that moves rapidly west into the Gulf.

Curry for Breakfast

Renee was a reasonably good cook — at least, we never saw her failures, which were tossed over the back fence for a family of feral pigs that used to come looking for food on a regular basis. She only ever cooked three different things for breakfast: steak and eggs, corned beef fritters and corned beef curry and rice, on a daily rotation. If they sound like strange choices for breakfast, consider what the local produce was: beef, beef and more beef. We had chickens, so we had eggs. Surplus eggs were preserved by greasing them with Vaseline and wrapping them in newspaper before placing them in the cold room. This method meant that the eggs would last almost indefinitely. The shells are porous, so the Vaseline seals the pores and helps prevent air from spoiling the eggs. The newspaper helps to keep a stable temperature around the eggs. The hens always went off the lay when the weather became hotter than normal. Normal was about 38-45 degrees Celsius.

Whilst doing the morning dishes one day, Renee and I spotted a solitary black feral piglet struggling along behind a sow and her other piglets. We looked at each other and agreed that it would probably die on its own, so Renee leapt over the fence and began chasing it. The little piglet squealed and put on an astonishing burst of speed. It ran into the generator shed and Renee made a dive for it, badly skinning her knees and elbows in the process. She caught the piglet and brought the squirming, squealing bundle, which had urinated all over the front of her T-shirt, into the house yard. We debated over what to do with it and came up with the brilliant idea of putting it in the sty with our domestic pigs. When Tom Dorrington heard, he hit the roof and told us of all the diseases a feral pig could pass on to domestic pigs. He marched straight down to the sty with his 22-gauge rifle and shot the feral piglet. So much for our heroic efforts.

As well as cooking for the family, and the home supervisor (me), Renee also had to cook for Mr D's brother and sister-in-law, and the four ringers — station hands — who ate with us at a long plank table with bench seats in the kitchen/dining room. The coarse table and benches dated from the time of the first Dorringtons on the property in the 1920s. Renee also had to prepare the tuckerboxes for when the men would be out in camp, too far from the homestead to come back for lunch or for the night. Her cakes were baked in large baking trays, desserts were cooked in several large bowls or another baking tray. Lunches in the homestead dining room were generally corned beef, boiled potatoes and boiled cabbage, with homemade bread. To cook in, Renee had the bulky old Aga woodstove with an oven on each side, and a gas stove for things that required a finer temperature control.

Having grown up on a nearby station, however, Renee was an expert in conquering the idiosyncrasies of the wood stove. I loved the corned beef curry and the corned beef fritters. The station denizens ate their way through six double loaves of home-baked bread every two days, which meant the air in the kitchen was permanently enticing with the fabulous aroma of large quantities of baking bread, which seemed stronger and more welcoming than any other fragrance emanating from the kitchen and is also the one which makes me most nostalgic. Mrs Dorrington taught me how to bake the six double loaves so that I could do it on the weekends. I really enjoyed the challenge and gradually developed forearms like Popeye.

Country cooks are very creative with limited ingredients, as the commonly used Country Women's Association and Schauer cookbooks attest. Sometimes, making beef taste like something else is the key to appeasing jaded palates. To this day, the Schauer cookbook is the one I tend to reach for first when planning a meal or want to make something a little unusual for a city cook.

The kitchen at Planet was made almost entirely of rough-hewn wooden planks, and had a separate walled-off area for washing up and storing the enamelled plates, bakeware and the battered tin pannikins from which we drank. The floorboards creaked with every footstep, which could be heard from the cook's room at one end of the verandah of the Main House. The Main House abutted the kitchen's verandah. The house was a wood and corrugated iron two-level building, and the kitchen building one storey. Renee had a sixth sense about people raiding the kitchen for any reason and would race down the stairs to challenge any night intruder into her territory.

Some evenings before bed, Renee and I would make ourselves an iced coffee — made of powdered milk and instant coffee, with no cream or ice-cream; they were pretty awful and these days the taste or texture of reconstituted powdered milk instantly reminds me of them. With hundreds of square kilometres of cattle, you'd think *one* of them would be a dairy cow!

Fresh fruit and vegetables were difficult to obtain. There was a homestead vegetable garden, but cattle nearby seemed to have a knack for getting in and cleaning up the plot. There was one cow I had seen which would sidle up to the two-metre-high vegetable garden fence, stand on its hind legs and neatly drop herself on the other side. Also, because of the extreme heat, there was a limit to what would grow there. Our main source of fresh produce was an infrequent visit by a refrigerated truck which travelled the hot and dusty road from Mt Isa through to Burketown and Normanton, stopping in at homesteads along the way. Mostly, our vegetables consisted of the kind that stored well: pumpkin, onions, potatoes and cabbage. For a few brief weeks there would also be fresh ripe turpentine mangoes straight from the tree to the cold room. They were small and stringy, but to us who were starved of fresh fruit and vegetables, they tasted like nectar of the gods.

MYO (Make Your Own) Fun

Without all of the mod cons, our entertainment was whatever we could make for ourselves, in the days before videos and DVDs, but we never designed anything that would hurt or embarrass anyone. Our main target was Tina's adult brother, Peter, who was forbidden on pain of death to make a play for either the cook or the governess (although once I had moved next door to Gregory Downs, he started to visit me).

One evening, after dishes and before lights out, we ran a fishing line from a hand reel down the verandah from Renee's room to Peter's. The line had a silvery plastic barramundi lure on the end, which we ran under his bed and hooked onto the sheet on the side closest to the wall. Our idea was to wait until we heard Peter climb into bed, then yank the sheet off with the lure, to give him a bit of a scare.

We heard the springs squeak as he sat on the bed, and waited a moment to pull on the lure. There was a piercing yell before we had even pulled it. We looked at each other in horror — Peter had stuck himself on the lure! We opened Renee's door and ran down to Peter's end of the verandah. Pushing open his door, we found — not Peter writhing in agony, but sitting up in bed, with the lure dangling from his fingers! 'I believe you ladies are looking for something?' he smirked.

You would have thought that we had learned our lesson. Not so. We spent the next couple of days trying to think up something even better. In the end, we decided on booby-trapping Peter's pride and joy, his yellow Toyota Hilux. We put an ancient piece of smelly Limburger cheese deep down in the glove box, greased the steering wheel with a mixture of Vaseline and garlic powder (Vaseline is good for lots of things!) and wired the leg of a road-killed kangaroo up underneath the chassis. It didn't take Peter long to find the cheese and clean the steering wheel, but although he looked and looked, he couldn't find the source of the dreadful smell coming from somewhere else. He had to tolerate the gag-inducing odour of rotting flesh until the leg finally fell off.

Peter knew that I hated frogs, which strangely, were in abundance at Planet Downs. I turned out my torch one night and lay down on the bed. Something cold and slimy touched my face, and I screamed. I turned on the torch again and found a large, fat green frog on my pillow. Mr and Mrs Dorrington came running, and with my face burning with embarrassment, I mumbled, 'Sorry — just a frog.' I used a shoe to catch it, carried it carefully to the front screen door and threw shoe and frog out the door as far as I could. I figured a shoe was more aerodynamic than a frog by itself, and would therefore travel further from me. I couldn't prove Peter had done it, but I had a fair idea it was him, when at breakfast the next morning, he said to me in the hearing of everyone there, 'You missed your big chance last night — if you'd kissed the frog he might have turned into a prince!' If you play practical jokes, you have to accept them in return. I also think it is a sign of personal acceptance that others feel they can joke with you without causing offense.

The very best practical joke I have ever heard of was perpetrated by a friend of a friend. Our mutual friend Frank was about to fly to France for a year's study. Trudy borrowed a wedding dress and veil, and bought a small bunch of flowers for her bouquet. She went to the airport, and just as Frank was about to pass through the security checkpoint, she ran through the terminal to him, calling out, 'Darling, darling, please don't leave me. How could you leave me at the altar like that?' Frank apparently turned every shade of red in existence, and more besides, and stammered to the people on either side of him, 'She's not my girlfriend, I hardly know her. I didn't do it.' That would have been an interesting flight because apparently a lot of people gave him a filthy 'How-could-you?' look. I am sure that was a send-off that Frank will never forget.

As children, we used to beg Dad to tell us again and again of some of the practical jokes that he and his brothers had played when they were youngsters. One of my favourites was the joke Dad and his brothers played on an elderly Chinese delivery man in their home town of Gulgong, NSW. The usually-drunk delivery man would peddle his wares and deliver shop orders with his vintage horse and wooden cart. Local children used to tease him a lot. He lost his temper with them occasionally, which only made it worse, because the children would then bait him until they had a reaction, and then happily go on their way. One evening, my father and his three brothers came across the old Chinaman, head nodding, drunkenly snoring on the seat of his cart, reins dangling loosely from his curled fingers. The horse was contentedly grazing on the sweet grass next to a post and wire fence. Dad and his brothers unhitched the horse, took it into the paddock on the other side of the fence, and hitched it up *through* the fence. Then they woke the poor man up. He couldn't figure out why his horse wouldn't go!

Dad and his three brothers all went to school in a small one-room school at the top of the hill behind my grandparents' house. Dad, who seems to have been the instigator of many of the Keyssecker brothers' pranks, ran a string from the school bell, under the floorboards, and up through a knot hole in the floor near his desk. Every time the teacher began to speak, Dad would give a quick, sharp tug on the string, ringing the bell. At the sound of the bell, all the children would rise to leave the room. The teacher would tell them to sit down, and the whole thing would be repeated. Needless to say, my dad received many a caning during his school years.

My practical joking was very tame on Planet Downs, compared with my later inventiveness.

CWA and Cricket

The main opportunity for women of the Gregory district to gather together was the convening of the monthly Country Women's Association meeting, held in the old corrugated iron hall at Gregory, opposite the pub (the only other building there at the time). Once the general business of the CWA meeting was over, it was a chance to renew friendships, chat and exchange recipes and ideas, try some new handcraft or other, and for the children to play together.

Some of the activities of the CWA included fundraising for local purposes such as amenities for the racecourse, or for specific pieces of equipment for the Royal Flying Doctor Service (RFDS). Others included handcrafts. I learned to do copper work there and produced a lovely little wall plaque of a woman dressed in 1920s clothing, cutting flowers in the garden. My mother has it still. I learned new knitting stitches, and was able to meet with governesses from other properties, and also meet the mothers of other children I heard every day on the School of the Air. Some of the women drove up to three hours with their families and governesses to attend the much-anticipated monthly meetings.

I became especially friendly with the two governesses

from Punjab station, Sara, who came from Ipswich, and Jackie, from Melbourne. They had the six Smythe children to teach between them, a very unusual situation. We shared ideas and teaching methodologies, and a lot of laughs.

One of the main drawcards of the CWA meetings was the food. Each of the women would come laden with cakes, buns, lamingtons, scones and more. In my own parody of the immortal words of Mary Poppins: supercalorific explodocious! It was all homemade and delicious. The mild-mannered CWA ladies became demons in the kitchen and used to try to outdo one another with their best recipes. It became a matter of pride that if Mrs A brought a sponge cake to one meeting, Mrs X would bring her version the next meeting, hoping to hear, 'Oh, these are the best scones/sponge cakes/lamingtons I have ever eaten.' Never would they concede defeat.

While the women had the CWA meetings, the men had cricket as a social get-together at the same time. It was played on the wide expanse of red dirt in front of the pub, encompassing the road, which at that point was ill-defined and about 50 metres wide, and the area in front of the hall, with one boundary marked by the 'prison tree'. That was where anyone arrested by the district policeman in the area's early days had been chained until the offender could be transported to Normanton lock-up. There was no actual police lockup in Gregory. Usually, there would be a cricket team from the Burketown district, Croydon or Normanton, against a team gathered together from the cattle stations in the Gregory District. The men would be dressed in immaculate whites at the beginning of the match, which grew redder by the minute until it looked as though they had rolled in the bright red bulldust.

The most unique feature of Gregory cricket, was the unofficial Cow Man on each team. The Cow Men stood one on either side of the match, to watch for cows, cars, road trains, trucks, small children and excited dogs, any of which might disrupt play. The Cow Men, who may also be women or kids, would yell 'cow!' or 'road train!' Play would halt temporarily while the teams moved to the side of the road, where they would wait impatiently for the intruder to pass and the dust to settle before resuming play.

When we returned home from one such CWA/Cricket day, there was an almighty storm. Tina was terrified and jumped up on the bed next to me, shaking with fear. The dogs were howling too. It has to be remembered that some years the wet season amounts to almost nothing, and there are children in the Outback who have never seen rain and are terrified of the accompanying thunder and lightning. I comforted her and explained in simple terms what was happening and that just because the storm was out of season, the same rules applied.

Mobile Disco

Renee had saved up enough money to buy herself a small second-hand car, and would no longer have to rely on one of her brothers to take her home to their property when she had time off. The car of her dreams was a little sky-blue Datsun. She wanted a good radio-cassette-player and so bought one by mail from a car accessories dealership in Mt Isa, our closest city. One of the ringers, Tony, said that he had experience in electrical wiring and could wire it into the car for her.

After Tony had finished the delicate task of marrying up the wires, most of the ringers, Tina's family and I all stood around holding our sides and laughing. When he turned on the radio, the inside light flashed in time with the music. Even after it had been taken out and redone properly, the car was forever known as the Mobile Disco.

After I'd been at Planet for about six months, Mrs Dorrington unexpectedly gave Renee and I permission to go to Mt Isa for a week. It was an exciting prospect, going back to civilisation. Neither of us had a great deal of money, so we decided to share a room for five nights at a dismal little boarding house in Camooweal Street. The first night we were there, the window was open and a large black cat jumped in, sniffing out the remains of our junk food chicken dinner, scaring the daylights out of us.

Not having seen traffic for so long, I actually felt scared to cross the road! Strangely, that fear has an actual name: 'dromophobia' — fear of crossing the street. We made the best of our time — haircuts, shopping, takeaway food, and movies... all the things that a city girl craved after months in the bush. I also had the opportunity to meet Tina's School of the Air teacher, and spend some time playing my mandolin with members of the Mt Isa Folk Club to which she and her husband belonged. It was wonderful. I was invited to play with them at the Rodeo Ball, for which they were providing the music. I was to sit beside their resident mandolinist and play — just exhilarating.

Before we left to return to Planet, we had decided to have a bit of luxury for our last night in Mt Isa. We booked two rooms at the Overlander Hotel — the best Mt Isa had to offer. I was in a room in the main section, and Renee was in another section. She had a little too much to drink at dinner that night, and I figured she would probably be a bit fuzzy-headed in the morning. I quickly worked out how the telephone system operated, and early in the morning, I asked the switch to put me through to Renee's room.

She answered the phone groggily, and I said, 'Good morning Miss Porter, this is Constable Bowen from the Mt Isa Police. You have been reported driving a car with stolen number plates. We would like you to come down to the Police Station at 8.30 this morning so we can examine the car.'

Fifteen minutes later there was a loud knock at my door.

When I answered her knock, a wild-eyed Renee exclaimed, 'That dirty rotten bastard has sold me a stolen car!'

'That's terrible! Didn't you check when you bought it?'

'No. I didn't think of anything like that. Now the police want me to go down to the Station. They said the plates are stolen.'

'Would you like me to come with you?'

'Oh, yes. I don't know how this could have happened!'

We were about two blocks from the Police Station before I could hold my laughter no longer and confessed. Renee was furious one moment, and burst out laughing the next.

'That was a good one. Boy, do I owe you!'

I had thought for a few moments that I was going to have to walk or hitch back to Planet. That car remained Renee's pride and joy for several years.

Outback Salute

It doesn't matter where in Australia you travel, you know when you have crossed the invisible borders and are in the Outback by the presence of three things: heat, dust and flies. The borders of the Outback may not be visible but it quickly becomes apparent when one is there. People in the Outback joke that you can become tired just from carrying the flies around. It is not really all that funny when you find yourself swatting endlessly at hundreds of small flies trying to drink your sweat, and entering your mouth, nose and eyes. I have only ever seen tourists wearing fly nets, not locals. And you will never see anyone in the Outback wearing the fabled hat with the dangling wine corks! Mostly people just put up with the flies, as they put up with the heat and the fine, clinging bulldust, because there is really no other viable option.

Some flies bite and others are just there to annoy. The biting flies leave large red welts that can remain painful for hours. If scratched at, the welts can become infected in a very short time. The flies are typically smaller than houseflies and like all flies, they seem to know when they are about to be swatted and escape unscathed just in the nick of time. This can make the swatting efforts all the more frustrating. They will also come back to the same spot half a dozen times in a row. Everyone who spends time in the Outback develops the Outback salute, flipping their hand continuously across their face to brush away the flies.

The flies do not only affect people, but also horses, cattle and dogs. Leaving a horse's forelock a little longer helped them keep flies out of their eyes. Horses and cattle swish their tails continuously from side to side to keep flies from their rear end. The only respite from flies comes at dusk, and that's when the mosquito squadrons turn out in force for attack.

The Grasshopper Plague

In the years that I spent at Planet Downs and Gregory Downs, the area was ravaged by a plague of large brown grasshoppers or maybe locusts. I hate grasshoppers, and doubly their larger cousins. They were everywhere and would congregate at night anywhere a light shone. For me, it put paid to reading in bed by torchlight after the generator was shut down. Even though the verandah was screened, somehow they managed to find their way in. Each morning I would have to sweep up what seemed like hundreds of their dead bodies from the verandah, the hall and the bedrooms. More than anything, I hated the way that they would cling to my hair and clothes when they landed on me. It is difficult to conceive of them as delicacies in some countries, but it makes sense — a kind of culinary revenge. They devastated the dry grass plains, and the little vegetable garden struggling next to the 'Second House'. Washing would dry with dozens of dark brown patches where the grasshoppers had landed, something Mrs D hated with a passion.

Knowing of my aversion to them, Tina, the ringers and Renee all conspired to put dead grasshoppers anywhere I might find them: under my pillow, in my cup, under a plate

... I even found one inside my mandolin! I took it all in good humour, but the more I reacted, the more they enjoyed it, so I hammed it up a few times just for their benefit. In my case, aversion therapy didn't work — I still hate them.

One night, Renee and I decided to go fishing after dinner, down at the Gregory River in our favourite swimming spot. We took a couple of truck inner tubes, blankets, fishing line with bait and lures, a torch, glasses and a bottle of wine. We lit a small fire, threw the blankets over the inner tubes (very comfortable seats), rigged our lines and opened the wine.

It was very still and quiet. The only sounds were the murmur of the water below the grassy bank, and the odd pop when figs from the overhanging Morton Bay fig tree dropped into the fire. Grasshoppers made a short 'ssss' sound as they suicided in the flames. We were looking forward to catching a feed of black bream or barramundi, at which Renee was an expert.

Suddenly, a large spiny grasshopper landed in my glass. I yelled, the glass ended up in the fire, I tangled myself in my fishing line, punctured the tyre tube and caught my hand on the lure, all in the space of a few seconds. Renee was laughing so hard I thought she would wet herself. It must have seemed like slapstick comedy from a play. We returned to the homestead with nothing but a funny story to tell. The fish swam freely for another night.

Grasshopper plagues are a routine annoyance in the Outback, and compete with the cattle and native fauna for food, inexorably eating any green thing in their path. They last for a month or more and are only rivalled by mice plagues in the damage they cause. Then one morning, the wind changes and they are gone. I was grateful that this was not a grain-growing area. The damage such pests cause to crops is devastating and complete.

Percy

One day Nancy, Tina's aunty, repainted the gate to the fence around the Main House. She painted it white so that it would show easily as it was often already dark before the men made it back to the homestead from a day out in the yards, or droving cattle on horseback.

There was a 1.5-metre-long goanna that we had seen entering the house yard by wriggling under the very gate Nancy had painted. He was nicknamed 'Percy' and tolerated on his daily visits. The goanna ended up with a crooked white stripe on its back from the wet paint. We had noticed that on some days the hens didn't seem to be laying as well as on others and it was attributed to the unrelenting heat.

'No, I reckon something's eating the eggs,' Mrs Dorrington Two said.

'Could be a snake, I s'pose,' replied Mrs Dorrington One.

'If it was a snake, it wouldn't be able to get out again after eating the eggs — it would be too fat to get through the chicken wire, or to go underneath it. There are broken eggshells, might be a goanna.'

'Hmm.'

The following day, while collecting the eggs and feeding

the chooks, I noticed grey-green Percy slinking around the back of the hen house with his peculiar side-to-side goanna gait, unmistakable with the white streak on his back. There was a section of chicken wire that had been pushed aside. Two and two were put together, and since Percy was the obvious culprit, he received a bullet for his trouble. Pieces of broken eggshell and the white stripe were all the evidence needed by the judge and jury to pass sentence. Egg yield improved noticeably over the next few days.

Country people are not sentimental in general about animals: they love their pets, but a sick animal will be put down with a mercifully quick bullet. Any animal that is affecting food production on the station will be relocated, if practical (such as a cow getting into the vegetable patch); dispatched, if not. A vet may be hundreds of kilometres away, and unable to come at short notice. Unless it was the grazier's most prized breeding bull, house calls were pretty much out of the question.

The only wildlife usually shot on sight were dingoes, feral pigs, goannas and dangerous snakes if they exhibited any sign of aggression or were too close to human habitation when encountered. Groups of young men used to come from Mt Isa for a weekend of 'pig shooting'. Pig shooters shoot for sport, but at the same time they do the graziers a service as feral pigs compete with cattle and native wildlife for food. They can also carry diseases which may definitely infect domestic pigs and possibly infect humans.

The Kill

I went out for the weekly kill with the boss and ringers once, out of curiosity because I wanted the whole station life experience. The beast they targeted from the mob was a cow about three years old. One cow would meet the needs of the station personnel three times a day for about a week. Steers (bullocks) and calves were never killed for home consumption as they were more valuable at market than cows, as they tended to grow larger. The larger the beast, the heavier it is and the more the grazier will be paid for it.

The stampeding cow was shot from the back of the moving Landcruiser tray-back, and dropped instantly, a great feat of marksmanship. When the men opened the cow's belly with the first few cuts, it was obvious that it was pregnant as a perfectly-formed bull calf foetus slipped out among the ruptured, steaming coils of intestines. It was too much for me.

It is normal practice for the cow to be skinned and roughly dismembered into its main joints, then brought back to the homestead on the tray-back of the Landcruiser on a bed of fresh eucalyptus branches. The gum leaves have natural eucalyptus oil which acts as an antiseptic, preventing the meat from becoming flyblown on the trip back to the homestead.

Back at the house, in the butcher shop, nicknamed 'the chop shop', the meat was further divided into other primary and secondary cuts. The legs were hung for a few days in the cold room, roasts were rolled and tied, brisket and other cuts were soaked in prepared brine tanks for making corned beef. Before being slid into the tanks, cuts for corning needed to have coarse salt rubbed into the meat by hand. The first time I had to do it, I almost threw up; the meat was still warm and twitching. However, I am a pragmatist — we need to eat, and food has to come from somewhere. With thousands of head of cattle, weather too hot to grow much, what else does one eat? Vegetarians need not apply.

After that first kill, I elected to stay behind and prepare the brine tanks and do the scrubbing and hosing out of the butchery each kill day. Some stations have a band saw in their butchery and can make cuts such as delicious T-bone and Y-bone steaks. Other stations achieve local acclaim for their homemade beef sausages. Our meals were supplemented with home-grown pork, ham and bacon, and the occasional barramundi or black bream from the nearby Gregory River, and on special occasions such as the birthday of one of the family, a chicken or two might be sacrificed.

Lessons Learned

As my job description included cleaning, I cleaned floors, windows, silver, rugs, lino, showers, toilets and dogs. One hot afternoon, after school had finished for the day and the siesta was over, Mrs Dorrington asked me to clean the louvres of both of the houses, and the men's quarters as well. This was expected to take a few afternoons to finish as almost every window at Planet had louvres. First, I started with hot, soapy water, then water containing vinegar/methylated spirits, and then polished them on both sides with months-old balled-up newspaper.

It took four solid afternoons of work to get them all done. By that time, I thought, 'If I never see another bank of louvres, it will be too soon.' The next afternoon we had an almighty dust storm that lasted for about two hours. The talcum-fine red dust penetrated every nook and cranny, and coated every surface including, of course, the freshly-cleaned louvres. I could have sat down and cried. Mrs Dorrington just shrugged and said, 'Get used to it.' And I had to start all over again.

After a while I settled into the rhythm of the Gulf and the pace of life there. People worked so hard and yet were laid-back at the same time. They spoke more slowly, and grinned more easily than their city counterparts.

It was not a case there of all men being equal. The Indigenous stockmen had their own quarters, and I rarely ever saw them except in the yards, doing chores around the house yard, or outside the pub. We had one married Aboriginal stockman who had three small daughters, and two unmarried men. I never saw inside their quarters, but assume they lacked a lot of the comforts we took for granted. Some of them did not even have glass on the windows.

The youngest daughter of Emmett Rockland, the married stockman, caught a bad cold, and despite help from the Flying doctor, died. I saw Emmett a few days later outside the pub.

'I'm really sorry to hear about your little girl, Emmett,' I said. He cocked his head to one side and replied, 'Tank you Missy. You the nicest white woman I ever met.'

People said of Emmett that if he'd been white, he'd have gone a long way. I found the attitudes towards the Aboriginal stockmen difficult to accept, until I was shown the other side of the picture as well and began to understand, if not agree with, the way things were.

The government dictated that cattlemen had to employ a certain number of blacks per whites. The owners would hire the Aboriginal stockmen who drifted from place to place, train them, teach them the parts of their craft that were lacking (most of the Indigenous stockmen were superb horsemen) only to have some of them go 'walkabout' the night before a major muster when all hands would be needed. Apart from men who had lived years in the district, many others could not be relied upon. The rules were that if a white stockman — ringer — did the same thing, he could be instantly dismissed, however, in the case of the Indigenous stockmen, their jobs had to be waiting for them when they returned from going walkabout. The attitude of the white ringers towards their black counterparts was generally one of restrained mateship. There was certainly admiration for the Indigenous way with animals, but there was resentment, too, over such rules. The ability to depend on one another in the bush can mean life or death and it was essential to be able to trust one's workmates.

There were also jobless Aboriginal families who lived in a collection of car bodies and plastic tarpaulins which rested on a slight rise above the other side of the bridge from the homestead, behind the Gregory Hotel. The place had been nicknamed 'Snobs' Hill'. Some of the ringers used to visit the women there at night. Those men were disparagingly known as 'jin jockeys'.

Emmett's wife, Linda, left behind when the men were out in camp, used to spend her time looking after her remaining two small daughters, as well as doing odd jobs around the homestead. One of the men used to tease Linda and whip her into a frenzied terror by telling her the Kadaitcha man was after her. The Indigenous people I met on the station were generally very quiet, kept to themselves and didn't interact with us 'whites' any more than was necessary. Most of them were superstitious. The threat of the Kadaitcha man was very real to them. The Kadaitcha man was a sort of witch doctor with special shoes made of feathers, human hair and blood. They were reputed to leave no footprints. Women and children were forbidden to even look at such shoes and they were usually kept in kangaroo skins or a specially-made pouch in the possession of one of the Indigenous men.

The Kadaitcha man was usually the man in the tribe whose responsibility it was to avenge unnatural deaths once the guilty party had been determined. These would be deaths believed to have been murder or the result of consultation with a witch doctor. As a rule, the Indigenous people of the north do not believe in death by natural causes. I do not know why Linda should be so scared of the Kadaitcha man, unless she thought that someone had willed her daughter dead. Indigenous health in the north is often precarious and their children can die of conditions which a white child would be able to shrug off. When the men were out in camp, Mrs Dorrington took pity on Linda and her remaining two daughters and let them sleep on mattresses on the wooden floor of the kitchen, near the wood stove at night. This seemed to give Linda some kind of peace of mind, having other people close by. I tried to get to know Linda a little, but she was so shy that she could hardly bring herself to look at me or answer if I spoke to her. She was the only black woman on Planet Downs, Emmett the only married black man there. She must have been lonely, just herself and the children in the ringers' quarters with the men away.

The station had two airstrips — a short, rough 'house' strip, and further out, a longer, better-maintained all-weather strip. This meant that the Flying Doctor used the house strip for most of his visits, but if the weather turned, he could still land on the all-weather strip.

My first winter in the Outback came as a complete shock. I had assumed it would be stinking hot all year round, and for the most part it was. However, the winter nights were unbelievably cold. The thermometer could drop below zero after a 38 or 42 degree day. I had brought very little winter clothing with me, and tended to put on just about all of it to go to bed. At one point, I had three blankets on the bed, and must have been a hideous sight in a long pink flannelette nightie, track pants, two pairs of socks, gloves, a beanie and a thick woollen scarf, but needed all of it. The mornings were also quite cool and required a jumper or jacket. I wore sheepskin boots quite a bit that first winter, much to the amusement of the ringers, a couple of whom nicknamed me 'Baa Baa'.

One night, after the generator had been off for about an hour or so, my door opened and in the dark, Tina's brother Ray whom I had not yet met, came in and sat on the end of my bed. I knew the family were expecting him sometime that night. He had just driven six hours from Mt Isa (known fondly by its residents and inhabitants as The Isa) and was obviously dead tired. His sister Joan and her baby were also in the house, as there was a family gathering that weekend.

'Where's the baby?' he asked.

'In the next room,' I replied, slightly puzzled. He said he had some food with him that needed to be brought in and placed in the cold room. 'I'll give you a hand, if you like.' I jumped out of bed and turned on my torch. He said in a shocked voice,

'Oh gawd, you're not Joan!' Apparently my room had been hers when she was younger and lived at home. As Ray and I were strangers, it was rather awkward, but he soon saw the funny side of it. We all laughed about it at breakfast the next morning. Joan asked him why he hadn't recognised my voice as that of a stranger. 'I was pretty tired after all day at work and then a six-hour drive, Sis. I think I can be forgiven for that.'

Have Sister – Will Travel

Whilst in the Gulf, I used to write home to my family to tell them what a great time I was having. The next thing I knew, I was back in Brisbane, and my younger sister Sandi had headed for the Gulf to become governess to four children on a fishing boat. She had started a career as a dental assistant, but like me, she wanted a change, a fresh challenge.

The fishermen sometimes had parties on the beach together with any other fishermen in the area. At one such party, Sandi met Jeff Newman, a barramundi fisherman. The next day, he motored for several hours in his dinghy just to have a cup of coffee with her. Romance soon blossomed and they went off together, and Sandi became first mate on a barramundi boat. They have been together now for about 27 years, and married twenty years ago. Since Sandi had to plan the wedding from such a long distance (they planned to marry at Bramston Beach near Cairns), everything had to be transported there. The dress she bought in Brisbane, the cake was ordered from Cairns, she had a DJ and a troupe of Polynesian dancers, caterers, and a trestle table groaning under the weight of about 150 cooked mud crabs as part of brunch the day after the wedding.

During the night before their beach wedding, there had been an almighty storm and as a result, there were deep sags in the marquee, and the dance floor was five centimetres under water. Fearing my sister's reaction, some of the men set to with wheelie bins and bailed it out. There was plenty of mud underfoot, and all including the bride rolled their pants up, hitched up their skirts, took off their shoes and had a damned good time regardless.

For my own role, I was the wedding photographer — 600 shots in three days (my gift to the happy couple), using three cameras, for a two-day wedding and the Hens' Night. I also hand-made 200 bonbonniere boxes and calligraphed each with Sandi and Jeff's names and the date, hand calligraphed all of the invitations, made the table centrepieces from bailer shells and flowers, and also made the bride's tiara in keeping with their 'ocean' theme, from gold wire, iridescent white beads like shiny grains of rice, two golden seahorses, a golden scallop shell and pearls. She looked lovely on the day. The reason they planned for a two-day wedding was that many people were coming from such long distances and it would make the trip more worth their while. Sandi and Jeff booked up every motel and caravan park in the district for their 200 guests. The second day of the wedding was very relaxed — caterers for brunch, cricket and other games on the beach, and a barbeque dinner. It was truly the best wedding I have ever been to and will have to elope if I ever marry, because there is no way I could top that.

Sandi and Jeff continue to profit from their barramundi fishing, although it is a hard life of broken sleeps, late night net checks, lots of fish gutting, and in Sandi's case, three days of seasickness whenever they first go out at the beginning of the season, which everyone else finds quite funny. They are passionate about creating sustainable fisheries and work with scientists to tag and release some species, to add to the pool of scientific knowledge about various creatures of Australia's northern seas and rivers.

Richard's Path

My brother Richard finished school at the end of Grade 10 and undertook a variety of jobs including working on a Brisbane River cruise boat, working for Mitsubishi at Toowong in Brisbane, as second-in-charge for Beaurepaires in Emerald before becoming Manager at Boral Tyres for which he worked remotely until opening a branch for them in Emerald (which was later sold to Bridgestone). He then ran a tyre business for the Swedish company Sandvik at Tomago near Newcastle, supplying tyres for underground mining vehicles.

Richard then moved to Canberra working for Komatsu (Mining and Construction Equipment) as Customer Support for ACT/Southern NSW. He then worked with Plant Assessors based in Newcastle who supplied Risk Management Services and looked after Ag Dealers and clearing sales around the whole of Australia. Now he works selling large vehicle tyres, and lives with his girlfriend Nina, west of Newcastle. I am very proud of the progress he has made.

Richard and his ex-wife Kerriann had two sons while they were living in Emerald, Mitchell and Brayden. The boys have grown into fine young men. Brayden is already married.

With his next position, Richard and Nina moved to a

semi-rural property west of Newcastle, large enough for Nina to have her beloved chickens, and a dog. The property has river frontage and some excellent camping, swimming and fishing spots. He has built a chute so that they are able to access the water for their canoes, as the bank is a stiff four-metre drop. They seem very happy there and my brother only has a short distance to drive to his new office. His company has been sending him all over the country to make presentations regarding their services. He has taken on the role with gusto and has made himself an indispensable employee in just a short time. His latest escapade was almost removing his leg with the chainsaw while cutting down a dead tree for firewood. He gashed his knee from side to side with it, but was extremely lucky as it was only a flesh wound. Crutches, nine stitches and a bit of uncharacteristic patience later, and he was as good as new. He joined my 'stitches in the knee' club (after my bilateral knee replacements). They have now settled permanently in Clarence Town, NSW.

FROM THE GULF TO JAPAN

The Big Adventure

As if going to live in the wild expanse of the Outback was not adventure enough, I calculated that by the end of my first year I would have enough saved from my $80 a week salary to visit Japan and meet my two penfriends. On the station, we were paid monthly, but the pay was generally merely a ledger entry to cash in the General Store there. I rarely had the need to spend any of my salary except for personal items. I seldom had to pay for a drink as the men were always wanting to buy me drinks at the pub, and I drank little anyway, preferring lemonade, or Coke, or the pinnacle of the publican's cocktail making skills, an exotic lemon lime and bitters. At that time, there were 400 yen to the Australian dollar. I had been offered the governess's post on Planet's neighbour Gregory Downs for the following year, so I had something to return to when Tina Dorrington enrolled in boarding school for the 1981 school year.

When I talked to Sara by radio two hundred kilometres away on Punjab Station and told her of my plans, she asked if she could come too. The question took me aback because I had always travelled alone and the idea of a travelling companion had simply never entered my head. She had a pen pal just outside Tokyo, as it turned out. We then spent half an hour each Saturday afternoon for weeks planning our trip and talking to each other over the Flying Doctor's two-way radio when it was free for general radio traffic. We met up at the Gregory Pub several times to finalise the details, including correspondence and bookings with various Youth Hostels, plane tickets, etc. It was very exciting, as we were young and neither of us had travelled overseas before.

By the time we left the Gulf at the beginning of December, just days ahead of the beginning of the wet season, we had the whole thing planned with military precision, with almost every eventuality mapped to the smallest details. Firstly, back to Brisbane in Sara's old car (surprisingly, with no mechanical or other difficulties) staying at pubs and in caravan parks along the way. I had no driver's licence at that time, so couldn't help with the driving. It was a long but uneventful trip. We paid for alternate tanks of fuel and split the cost of rooms at a pub or van park each night. Luckily, we had no collision with any wildlife other than a small stray bird, and generally avoided driving at dusk and dawn, when kangaroos and other wildlife are most active. After four days, we arrived back in Brisbane. We went our separate ways to catch up with friends and family, and to purchase some cold weather clothing. Winter clothes were very difficult to find in Brisbane in mid-summer, so we had to resort to second-hand coats and woolly hats. The day of our departure rolled around quickly. Sara and I were both so keyed up the night before that we barely slept. We departed at 10 pm from Brisbane International Airport where the roar of jets landing and taking off added to our excitement.

I had a penfriend in Hiroshima and another just outside Kyoto. With Sara's penfriend near Tokyo, we had a clear direction from Tokyo in the east, west to Hiroshima. I didn't particularly want to see the three smaller islands at that point, and Sara was also happy to remain on Honshu, the main island. One thing we stipulated to our penfriends was that we wanted to see snow. We also wanted to see the everyday life of Japan, including police stations, schools, fire stations, shopping centres and hospitals. This request really puzzled our Japanese friends who expected that, as tourists, we would just want to see tourist attractions such as shrines and temples. One or two shrines and temples are enough to satisfy a tourist, as the special features and minor differences among them are wasted on *gaijin*.

We were treated to a special sight as the plane banked over Tokyo in the early sunrise — Mt Fuji in all its glory. As the pilot announced that it could be seen from one side of the plane, there was a crush of passengers rushing from the opposite side of the plane, with cameras clicking at every available window and cries of '*subarashii! Suteki*' and many 'oohs and aahs'. It was glorious in pinks, reds and apricots, its beautiful symmetrical cone rising starkly from the plain. It was also a sight we had been warned that, because of the heavy smog over Tokyo, we would probably never see. This seemed like a very good omen. Walking from the terminal to the outside was like being body-slammed into a brick wall. It literally took our breath away. Sara and I wondered if we could survive the cold after travelling from 45-degree heat to minus three in Tokyo.

My first encounter with a Japanese toilet evoked dismay first and puzzlement second. I had to actually leave the toilet and whisper in Sara's penfriend Akiko's ear, 'Which way do I face?' I had a bad right knee, strapped and stiff, so things that one would normally take for granted, such as the squat toilets, stairs for which the Japanese have a mania, and sitting Japanese-style with our legs tucked under, were extremely difficult for me. I quickly learned the Japanese for, 'I'm sorry I can't sit Japanese style, I have a knee injury'.

In Chiba, we had a wonderful time with Akiko's family. They spoke no English, except for Akiko, so she was kept busy as our interpreter together with my halting Japanese. Thankfully, they understood and were politely amused by my linguistic efforts. The family lived close to the beach, and we all meandered down for a look. It was the first time I had seen a beach with *black* sand! The sand was volcanic rutile. Wave height was a little over five centimetres — no surfboards here! No wonder Japanese tourists are crazy for our pristine gold and white sandy beaches. On the other side of Tokyo, we travelled to Yokohama bay, with its amazing array of huge container ships, bulk carriers and smaller craft. We indulged in hot *taiyaki*, a cross between a fritter and a cake, containing sweet, red bean paste. They were delicious and known as Yokohama's *meibutsu* (the culinary specialty of an area). When Japanese visit other towns or cities in Japan, their family and friends expect to be given *meibutsu* on their return. Most railway stations, and the airports have stalls and shops selling *meibutsu* from different regions in the country — just in case the traveller has forgotten to buy them when they were actually in those areas. They are almost always packed in wrapped boxes and placed in carry bags for ease of travelling. Japanese are very careful in the way they wrap gifts and ordinary purchases. One of my Dutch friends told me that he had even had his purchase of chewing gum wrapped! Even the Japanese would admit to that being a little extreme.

As it was the time of university holidays, Sara's penfriend was able to accompany us to Kanazawa on the Japan Sea coast. We had all the snow we could possibly want, so much that the taxi could not drive up the driveway to our accommodation because of the slippery driveway. We had to manhandle our bags from the foot of the hill up the icy slope in gathering darkness at 3.30 pm to the Youth Hostel where we were to stay for a few days. As soon as we had registered and dumped our bags, Sara and I dashed outside to play in the snow. We had a quick snow fight, hurriedly built a snowman with an extra ball of snow at each ear, took a few photos, then rushed inside to sit by the large open fireplace of the best Youth Hostel I have ever seen. It was like a five-star ski lodge.

Akiko asked, 'What kind of snowman is *that?*'

We smiled and replied, 'A koala, of course!'

I loved the silence of the snow and the feeling of being cocooned in virginal white. However, when I lived in Japan, I came to appreciate snow in the best possible way, as a nice view from a warm room. The large feather-like flakes that seem to fall so slowly to earth were something of which I have never tired.

Our pen friends welcomed us with open arms and homes. We stayed just one night with each, knowing that space was at a premium and we were probably ousting someone from their room to stay there. The rest of the time we stayed in Youth Hostels and *minshuku*, a budget version of a Japanese-style inn, which we had booked from the Gulf, nearly four months earlier. The itinerary we had mapped out included Chiba, where Akiko lived, Tokyo, Nagoya, Kyoto, Osaka, Kanazawa and Hiroshima. One or another of our pen friends and their friends were able to accompany us for different parts of our journey which removed a great deal of the stress and confusion we might otherwise have faced. Without the later ease of computers with which to do our bookings, everything was done by mail and international reply-paid postcards, with an average turn-around time of four weeks, even if responses to our requests were written and posted the day they were received.

Everything we saw was new to us and Sara and I must have been very easy to spot as first-timers. I had kept up my high school Japanese over the two-way radio as there was a Japanese man who lived on a station near Borroloola, just over the border in the Northern Territory. It was very handy and I managed to get us out of more trouble than in. The Japanese we met were amused by Sara's name. It means plate or dish in Japanese.

Kanazawa town, below the Youth Hostel, was interesting. Something that made me laugh was the sight of a Colonel Sanders dummy dressed as Santa Claus, outside a Kentucky Fried Chicken outlet. My uncle Ian back in Brisbane worked as an area manager for the chain, so I took a photograph, knowing it would amuse him. We had four days in Kanazawa.

As we were there for Christmas Eve, and apart from ourselves, there was only one other guest, the managers of the Hostel invited us all to join them in front of the fire, for some *Kurisumasu Keeki* — Japanese Christmas cake, always eaten on Christmas Eve, a sponge cake covered in artificial cream and decorations of Santa, Christmas trees, and maybe reindeer. By Christmas Day, all Christmas cakes have disappeared from the shops and New Year specialties are in. Unmarried Japanese women are derisively known as Christmas cakes — no one wants them after the 25th.

Backtracking from Kanazawa to Tokyo, we took the *Shinkansen (*Bullet Train) to Kyoto. Once again, we saw Mt Fuji. It was a rare, clear day, and every bit as beautiful as a picture postcard. We were told again how lucky we were to see it. Most of the time, Tokyo smog and cloud obscure the summit. 'On a clear day you can see Mt Fuji' doesn't happen very often.

Kyoto and Nara

Nara was a lovely place with what seemed like a plethora of parks and gardens, but it is most famous for its deer. They are incredibly tame, to the point of being a nuisance. If we sat to take a drink from our flasks, the deer would be all over us, pushing their noses into our hands and faces, looking for handouts of food. I had never seen deer in the flesh before, and I have to confess, not having had venison before, I was mentally comparing them with beef cattle, and wondering how they tasted!

We saw quite a lot of snow in Kyoto — I couldn't get enough of it! After a dry year in the Gulf with weather operating in only two modes: hot and dry or hot and wet, it was just beautiful! The Temples of the Gold and Silver Pavilions and their surrounding gardens were magnificent. It was easy to imagine the splendour of the gardens in spring, summer and autumn as well. Gardens in Japan are usually designed to take full advantage of each season. Having seen quite a bit of Japan now, I still think Kyoto is my favourite city. The contrast between ancient and modern, side by side, was sometimes breathtaking. For example, I saw ultra-modern three-wheel cars in a showroom, and in the narrow street in front, a very old woman dressed in *mompe*, traditional peasant women's clothing consisting of quilted trousers and overshirt, pulling an ancient handcart loaded with hand-made wooden crates.

As we needed a public toilet, Sara and I looked around and couldn't find one, so I suggested we walk into the Imperial Hotel near the Kyoto Railway Station like we owned the place, and use the toilets there. They were cleaner than most public toilets in Japan, had gold tapware, and black marble, with only western toilets. Very opulent. I opened the door of one of the cubicles and burst out laughing.

'Sara, come and see this!'

'What is it?'

'Have a look for yourself.'

She, too, burst out laughing. There were clear footprints on either side of the seat of the western toilet in the cubicle. Older Japanese are not familiar with western toilets and try to squat above them as they would over a Japanese toilet. I could just imagine some little old lady hoiking up her layers of *kimono* and clambering up on the seat, mentally cursing westerners for their damn fool design for toilets.

The temples and shrines in Kyoto are some of the best and most well-known in Japan. The trek up the hill to Kiyomizu is worth the effort for the view alone. Kiyomizu temple is built suspended out over a densely-wooded valley. I found it hard-going sometimes with my knee not cooperating fully, but persevered. Even for a non-Shintoist, non-Buddhist, the atmosphere of the shrines and temples was usually quiet and very peaceful. Most Japanese will say they are both Shintoist (for weddings) and Buddhist (for funerals and ancestor worship). About 0.9% are Christian and other religions. If the statistics are added together, it is more than one and a half times the population of Japan. Most sects of Buddhism and Shintoism do not overtly proselytise. One Buddhist sect in particular, however, is known for its militancy — the *Sokka Gakai* — actively seeking to recruit new members. In the past 20 years, it has been active in Australia, and not all of its members are Japanese.

In Kyoto, too, there was an abundance of Japanese restaurants offering authentic-looking and appetising Japanese meals, if the plastic renditions in the windows were anything by which to judge. These plastic facsimiles of meals make great (if expensive) souvenirs. Sara and I became very good at collaring a waiter or waitress, and getting them to accompany us into the cold, so we could point to what we wanted. I learned the names of lots of different dishes, as I would get the waiter or waitress to write down the name of the dish in both *kanji* (complex characters originating from Chinese) and *hiragana* — simple Japanese characters, and in this way built up a small notebook with food-related names and phrases.

We spent just over five days in Kyoto, and were able to visit Uzumasa, which is a kind of Japanese version of Movie World. It is set up as an ancient Japanese village, complete with red-light district, gracefully arched bridges, and taverns. We took the opportunity to dress up in period costume, including the heavy *katsura* (wig) which weighs over a kilogram, to have our photos taken. People wandered around the village as *samurai*, *o-iran*, and *geisha*, posing for photos with visitors.

There was also a demonstration of how well-choreographed sword fights are in old-style Japanese movies. Rather than waning in popularity over the years, such movies are now enjoying a resurgence in popularity and sometimes even have a cult following.

At Uzumasa, I had my photo taken with a shorter chubby Japanese fellow dressed as a samurai complete with *chonmage* which is the shaved patch on the head with the rest of the hair pulled back and flipped over the bald pate, like an inverted ponytail. I sent the photo home with the writing on the back reading, 'Hi Dad, this is my new boyfriend,' just to stir him up.

The Youth Hostels where we mostly stayed varied a great deal in set-up, size and facilities. The most, ah, unusual (I am being kind here) one we stayed in was in Onoda, a suburb of Osaka. It was a two-storey fairly ordinary but run-down Japanese house. There were two rooms for guests: one downstairs for men and one upstairs for women. It was freezing and we wondered how we could possibly warm up. There was no heater in the room with traditional paper and glass screens, wood and paper walls, and rice straw *tatami* mats on the floor. The elderly lady who ran the 'hostel' told me in Japanese that we had to be out the next morning by 8.00 am, and that we must take our valuables with us so that *doroboo* would not break in and steal them. Not very reassuring!

Sara was beginning to feel the effects of a cold, and quickly unfolded her *futon*. We were puzzled by the presence of a large blue plastic tub in the middle of the floor of our room. I asked the old lady about it. She pointed to the ceiling and said just one word, '*ame*' (rain)! She must have taken pity on us, because just as I made myself comfortable, I heard, '*Oi, chotto unta*' (hey you up there).

'*Hai,*' I descended carefully to the bottom of the impossibly narrow stairs. She handed me something metal that looked like a large, squashed hand grenade. It was a hot water bottle.

'Well Sara, I think you need this more than I do. It looks like one between two.'

I settled myself again and again I was summoned '*Oi, chotto unta*' (please don't use this — it is *not* polite Japanese). At the bottom of the stairs she handed me another hot water bottle. We were very grateful for even the minimal warmth they afforded and buried them deep down in our futons.

Spending time in Japan as a tourist was very enjoyable, but for me it played another role. A couple of years later, the opportunity to move to Japan to live presented itself. Having had a taste of the country already, it made me understand a little more of what I was getting myself into. However, visiting and living somewhere are two entirely different things, as I would discover.

Shoe Cream and Cow Piss

Most people know that the Japanese eat some bizarre things that other cultures do not necessarily recognise as food items. For example, they eat eel, sea cucumber, jellyfish, pickled white radish — *takuan*, fermented soya beans, whale and horse meat. A Japanese boss I had in later years commented that 'Japanese eat everything out of the sea except gravel, and anything on four legs except tables and chairs.'

Sara and I were introduced to a dizzying array of strange and wonderful foods, some of which I preferred *not* to know the origins. The Japanese have a saying that, *For every new food you try, you live another hundred days.* The two of us are now likely to live very long lives!

Having just come from cattle properties in North Queensland, we were shocked to be offered glasses of cow piss to drink. We stared at it and just looked at each other — it was an opaque white and certainly didn't smell like cow piss. Who would have thought the Japanese would go so far as to drink that? Akiko (Sara's pen friend) explained that it was made from fermented milk and sugar and was called *Calpis*. We had trouble trying to stop laughing, but laughed until tears ran down our faces. I tried to explain that that was not what we thought we had heard. I don't think Akiko quite understood why we were laughing, but politely joined in anyway.

We were astounded at the wide variety of 'bending machines' (*jidoohanbaiki*, literally 'automatic sell machine') as there is no 'v' sound in the Japanese language. One could buy almost anything from them: hot drinks, cold drinks, clean underwear, alcohol, pornographic magazines, hamburgers (yes, that's right!) and to my delight, being a sucker for anything with custard, boxes of fresh, custard-filled choux pastries. In Japan, they are called *shuu kuriimu*, which we heard as 'shoe cream'. Again, we had wondered what we were about to be offered.

In our suitcases, we had brought small jars of Vegemite, to offer our hosts to see if they liked it. Most of them thought it was chocolate spread, and layered it on thickly and all but spat it across the room when they tasted it. Then again, I have a Japanese friend who asks for Vegemite to be sent to him sometimes, as his family like to put it on their rice. It is similar in taste to a Japanese seaweed preparation that some Japanese like on rice — both are dark in colour and salty.

I loved Japanese breakfasts. They consisted of *miso* soup, made from fermented soya beans, a bowl of hot rice, a whole grilled fish (cold — as most establishments grill the fish part of their breakfasts the night before), a raw egg, some salad and some strips of *nori* seaweed. There is a great art involved in manoeuvring all of the elements into position. The raw egg is cracked into a bowl, and whisked lightly with chopsticks, then poured onto the bowl of hot rice. A strip of *nori* is placed on top of the hot rice and egg mixture and bent downwards with the tips of the chopsticks until the two short sides meet around a portion of rice and is then conveyed to the mouth. The process is repeated until one either runs out of *nori* or runs out of rice. All elements of the meal should be finished at the same time, so it is only with practice that one can balance all of the dishes and demonstrate that one understands and appreciates this aspect of Japanese culinary etiquette. It is important to note that one may leave amounts of any other food but rice. It harks back to famine and wartime when the most basic food — rice — was scarce. To leave rice in the bowl is to show bad manners. Sara, on the other hand, preferred fruit and yoghurt. Some of our Japanese friends would settle for toast and tea.

Japanese food must be approached with an open mind. My grandmother visited Japan as part of a cruise that visited Japan long before I had the chance to go there. I asked her where she had stayed and what she had eaten. She replied that they had stayed in western-style hotels and eaten western food. What a waste of the possibilities! Perhaps the organisers thought that was what westerners wanted. Food and culture are such a major part of the experience of a foreign country, that I felt sorry she hadn't had that opportunity. Sara and I were lucky to have our pen friends and their families who took such delight in showing us firsthand their culture and cuisine.

Our accommodation varied enormously during our month in Japan but the strangest of all was the sick room of a school that was in recess! One of our friends knew the guard and he sneaked us in to sleep on the examination tables. It had everything that a small hospital examination room would have. The novelty quickly wore off, however, as the examination tables were very hard and uncomfortable, but to use the magic word to the ears of travellers on a shoestring, it was FREE.

Homeward Bound

After a couple of days in Hiroshima seeing my pen friend Yoshiko and some of her friends, we were ready to fly home from Osaka to Brisbane after our month in Japan. The Hiroshima Peace Park's museum was closed when we were there, a relief in some ways, as I have been told it is very confronting. The park itself on a very cold, overcast winter's day was beautiful in a desperately grim sort of way, with the 'Atomic Dome' holding sway over everything else in the park, visible from almost every location. It had originally been a weather observatory and was one building in Hiroshima that was never rebuilt. The war is something that is not discussed in Japan.

We had had a wonderful month and couldn't believe the trip had gone so well with no major hiccups or problems; attributable largely to our friends there. Most of the Japanese I had met in Australia were lovely, and so were the Japanese in their home country. This was one factor that influenced my later decision to return to Japan to live. It was sad saying goodbye to everyone and to pack up for the flight home. The whole trip had cost us around $2000 each (including airfares). Sara and I had had a wonderful time, seen the things we wanted to see, picked up a load of souvenirs for friends, relatives and ourselves, as well as enough funny stories to dine out on for months. It's a good thing that we both had a similar sense of humour and were able to laugh at ourselves.

GREGORY DOWNS

Gregory Downs

Sara went on to another governess position in south-west Queensland, and I returned to the Gulf, to my new post at Gregory Downs.

Gregory Downs Hotel used to be a stop for coaches and horses travelling between Burketown in the north-west, and Mt Isa to the south. The Gregory was one of many stops along the way, and grew to be the hub of the whole Gregory district. There was originally a small general store there as well as the pub. The original homestead used to be on the same side of the river as the Hotel, but visitors became a nuisance and so it was relocated to the opposite side of the river, reached only by a narrow wooden bridge. The buildings on the homestead consisted of one two-story house for the manager, his family, and the governess, a small cottage for the head stockman and his wife (if he had one), men's quarters, an ablution block for the family and one for the men, and a separate kitchen building. Kitchens were built separately on many stations so that if there was a fire in the detached kitchen, the most likely place for one to start, there was less chance of it destroying other buildings. With a dearth of pressurised water and no chance of a fire engine, it was preferable to lose just the kitchen than to lose the whole of the manager's accommodation as well.

Tancreds, a large meat company, owned Gregory Downs at that time. Rather than a family concern, it was in the care of the Manager, Robbie McDowall. That it was run somewhat differently than Planet Downs was evident in many ways, both large and small. For example, the generator was run for most of the day and into the early evening; there were extra staff — a grader driver for maintaining tracks, roads and airstrips, more Indigenous ringers, extra white ringers, and later during the year, a new head stockman and cook for the men. Gregory was larger than Planet Downs. The three combined stations of Gregory, Planet Downs and Yeldham were capable of running around 24,000 head of cattle when they were first settled as one property in the late 1870s.

I was happy to be remaining in the same area for a second year as I now knew most of the people from the district. My new charges were Tracy aged 8, Penny 6, and Bronwyn 3. Robbie's wife Veronica did most of the cooking for the station in the early part of that year, and could not handle the children's education as well, which is why they opted for a governess to both teach the children and help around the homestead.

One of my jobs was to feed the pigs and chickens. I became quite attached to one of the sows who would waddle up to me and nuzzle my hand. She had just three piglets (pigs usually have up to twelve piglets) and then died suddenly of suspected puerperal fever. I undertook to feed and care for the three little piglets, one female and two male. I called them Peter, Paul and Mary after the popular folk music group. At night they slept in a fruit box on the verandah outside my room so I could feed them during the night in relative comfort. Mary managed to get out of the box one morning, and as I was washing up the morning dishes downstairs, I saw a pink blur falling from the upper level of the house. I raced outside to see what it was and saw Mary, quite dead from the fall. As for the two male piglets, one was long and skinny and the other was short and fat, so I renamed them Laurel and Hardy after the comedians of similar proportions. After a couple of weeks of intensive care and frequent feeds, they were big enough to be reintroduced to the pig sty and they thrived there. Later on they became pork chops, hams, bacon and ribs — all delicious.

The Flying Doctors ran fortnightly medical clinics at Gregory, for everyone in the district — anyone within driving range was welcome, no appointment necessary — made possible by fundraising and public donations. If you have the chance to donate to the Royal Flying Doctor Service, it will be much appreciated by those who live in isolated areas with no access to any other medical care. Each homestead has a special large metal first aid box supplied by the Royal Flying Doctor Service. Everything in the kit is labelled and numbered. If the FD is giving medical directions over the two-way radio during his daily radio clinic, he would say something like, 'Take two of Number 51, twice a day'.

I had need of the Flying Doctors' clinic when still living on Planet Downs. It was the weekend of the Races and Race Ball. Greg, a friend of the family from Mt Isa had arrived that afternoon and offered me a lift to the Ball in his new ute. He let his girlfriend drive, and she almost hit a kangaroo on the way.

'Stop the car. I'll drive the rest of the way,' he said in alarm.

Karen opened her door to let Greg (sitting in the middle) out, and I opened mine as well. I caught the heel of the first pair of high heels I had worn in two years in the hem of my long, cream, silk-jersey gown. As I fell I twisted and landed backside first in the bulldust at the verge of the road. No matter how much I brushed it down with my hands, I still had a red bullseye covering my bum. The other two laughed, thinking it hilariously funny.

I noticed that during the Saturday night of dancing that the little finger on my left hand was very sore. It swelled to the size of a pork sausage, so a little concerned, I saw the doctor on the following Wednesday.

'Clive, I don't know what I've done to it but it is really sore.' He took one look and said, 'Ha ha, you've broken it. How did you do it?'

'You wouldn't believe me if I told you.'

'Try me.'

'I fell out of a stationary car on the way to the ball — and I hadn't touched a drop.'

He replied that it was definitely 'one for the books' and that he'd not heard anything so funny in a long time.

I was flown in the Flying Doctor's plane to Mt Isa to have the finger X-rayed and set in a metal splint. It was broken in two places. That's what you get when a heavy object lands on delicate bones. I had to stay a few days there until someone from Planet was able to come and fetch me, when they had business which took them to The Isa.

The FD holds a daily radio clinic session for up to an hour each weekday morning, during which people from outlying stations from Mt Isa may call in over the two-way radio and describe their symptoms to the FD who would then advise them on what to do. Later, when I was living at Gregory, Veronica used to have the radio turned up loud while working in the kitchen, for entertainment. She always knew who in the district had what ailment. This was a practice frowned upon because it was deemed to be impinging on patients' privacy, but it's a bit difficult to keep the radio calls private when they are broadcast over hundreds of square kilometres!

One morning, during the period when telegram messages were being read over the radio, I heard news of my paternal grandfather's passing. I was very sad that I had not had time to get to know him better, but he'd been a taciturn man, not given to lengthy conversations. Because of time and distance, I was unable to go to the funeral, which was held in his home town of Gulgong, western New South Wales.

School Under the Stairs

Life for me on Gregory Downs quickly settled into a comfortable routine of teaching the children, preparing their lessons, cleaning, and feeding the pigs and chickens. I had volunteered to cook on Saturdays to give Veronica a day off each week. I loved cooking, so it was no hardship. I learned quite a lot from her, and became a pretty good bread maker, large-quantity cake baker and made a mean roast. The kids, and sometimes one or two of the men, would come into the kitchen to sit and chat as I worked.

The girls' uncle and Robbie's brother John was the head stockman for most of the year I was there. His childhood nickname had been 'Rat' because he had a bad habit of chewing on the horse's reins while riding. The children called him 'Uncle Rat'. I never heard him called John. Because the children were quite young and had difficulty with my surname, we settled on 'Miss K' for me as having just the right combination of respect and familiarity.

The schoolroom on Gregory Downs was a built-in area under the external stairs to the upper floor. Three sides of the room were louvered (more louvres!) with one side abutting the side of the dining room that had louvres. There was no door, just a token piece of corrugated iron pulled across the doorway in an attempt to keep the two station dogs and assorted crawling things out. There was just enough head room for me, and squeezed together, three small desks and four chairs. There was a rickety blackboard nailed to a pillar; it used to wiggle backwards and forwards on the rare occasions there was a breeze, or whenever I wrote on it.

Tracy was on remedial work as well as her standard Grade 3 lessons. I quickly realised that not only did she have a good memory, but she was very intelligent. I wrote to the Distance Education teacher in Brisbane and discreetly asked why she was on remedial work. Her mother Veronica had taught her in Grades 1 and 2, she replied, and with all the other work she had to do on the station, had skipped chunks of the basics. With the teacher's approval, I took Tracy right back to basics and would daily spend extra time with her. She not only caught up, but topped her class that year. I was very proud of her and her parents were very happy. Sometimes it is wise to listen to gut instinct and I like to hope that it made a difference to Tracy for the rest of her life.

Penny was not such an apt student. She was easily distracted by things happening outside the classroom especially when the men and cattle were in the yards across from the house. It was very difficult to keep her engaged in what she was supposed to be doing. She was stubborn, more so than any other child I have ever met! I found that with her, I had to divide tasks into short, punchy sessions, rather than whole lessons at one time.

Penny was the most loving of the three girls. She was very

free with hugs, and was always looking for special things to show me. On the rare occasions when I would go away for a few days or a week, she would be the one of the children who greeted me the most effusively on my return. I guess I developed a bit of a soft spot for Penny because I saw a little of myself in her.

Bronwyn, the three-year-old, was bright and could actually handle quite a bit of the work of the Grade 1 curriculum. I tried to theme each week's lessons around one of the girls' printed lessons to bring their learning together and give them more of a class atmosphere. I introduced handcrafts at different levels that would tie in with their lessons, physical education, and music. Penny introduced biology. One afternoon the girls were standing around outside, laughing. I walked over to see what they were so taken with, and found a dead frog on the concrete.

'Did you girls kill that frog?' I asked, prepared to be angry.

'No, Miss K, just watch!' they answered gleefully.

Lo and behold, the frog flipped over after a couple of minutes and hopped away. They told me that Rocket frogs play dead as a defence strategy. The children were keen observers of the natural world around them and I learned a great deal from them.

As part of her lessons one week, Tracy was required to write a story about a circus. I was incensed. There was no supporting material, nothing to tell the children what a circus was! These were bush children who saw at most the same thirty people a year, had never seen circus animals, a big-top or known what the atmosphere in that big-top could be like. For the whole week, I tailored the lessons around circus activities, artwork, magic tricks and dressing up like clowns. At the end of the week, we gathered the parents and some of the ringers together to put on a circus show of our own. Even their pet Dachshund Mary-Lou was dressed up with a frill around her neck and a party hat on. Efforts were made to teach Mary-Lou to jump through a hula hoop, but she was a dismal failure. Nevertheless, she had the ability to set the children off in peals of laughter. The kids loved it. The parents were impressed, and after that, the kids could say, 'Yes, I have some idea of what a circus is.' I wrote to Distance Education and suggested that they may be able to include supporting materials in future if the lessons were to be set around unfamiliar topics. Unfortunately, I am sure not all home supervisors would have the ability, resources, enthusiasm or time to be as creative and make it as real for the children.

Once a month, lessons involved taping a particular section of a lesson in a question and answer format, to send to the Distance Education teachers. Penny and I were working through basic punctuation.

'Penny, can you tell me what a full stop means?'

She thought about it for a moment, then said, 'It means pull up an' 'ave a blow'.' It was all I could do not to laugh out loud. 'Pull up and have a blow' in Outback vernacular means exactly that — stop and have a rest. There was another time when she announced out of the blue, 'Miss K, butterflies have feathers'. I asked her how she knew that and she replied indignantly, 'They've got *wings.*' When one considers that cherubim and angels are usually depicted with bird-feather wings, maybe her reasoning was not flawed at all. She was more of a bush kid than the other two put together, and had a unique perspective on the world.

When not out in the yards, the old Blue Heeler cattle dog, Blue, used to lie on the concrete outside the classroom in the little shade the stairs afforded. Mary-Lou also enjoyed the cool of the shade next to the classroom. She believed she was a cattle dog, and would run in amongst the milling cattle in the yards and nip at their heels whenever there were any in the home yard. Blue's claim to fame was that any time he was on the back of the Toyota, he would snap at overhanging branches until he unintentionally latched on, falling out of the truck on many occasions. The driver would have to stop, pick up Blue, throw him back into the truck and keep going. If too far from the homestead, he would be unable to walk the distance back on his own. The standard cry was, 'Bloody Blue — he's fallen out again'.

Some of the things the kids did really stirred my curiosity. One of those things was to pick bush lemons (not as sour as their Lisbon cousins), grab a saltshaker and suck on the salty flesh of the lemons. I was completely bemused to see them do something so un-child-like. Most children hate sourness and infinitely prefer sweet tastes.

One Monday, I started to read to the girls three chapters each day of Osmar White's wonderful children's book series, *The Super Roo From Mungalongaloo*. It was about Dr McGurk and his trusty camel, Cathy, crossing the dreaded Deadibone Desert, and the antics of the Super Roo, a crusader for conservation. To make it more interesting, I read the spoken parts in character voices which the children absolutely loved and would clap and giggle at my efforts. The two dogs outside would prick up their ears at the different voices, too. They were probably wondering how these other people had managed to get past them. These books remain a favourite series of mine, but are unfortunately now out of print.

Snake!

From infancy, bush children are taught to have a healthy fear of and respect for snakes. This is just as well, because the Gulf is home to some of the world's deadliest snakes. A bite from a Taipan, Great Western Brown, Tiger Snake or Red-bellied Black Snake can often mean death because anti-venene can't be obtained in time to save the victim's life. The Flying Doctor can't always arrive in time and the nearest hospital, as in our case, was more than 120 kilometres away.

Every time I used a shower on someone's property in the Gulf, there was a broomstick in the corner of the shower recess. When I first arrived at Planet I asked what it was for. There was no grate over the drain hole. 'It's for snakes,' I was matter-of-factly told. Thereafter, I always entered the shower with double trepidation — frogs AND snakes!

One morning the children and I were removing the corrugated iron 'door' from the classroom, when Penny pulled out her chair to sit down. Suddenly, she uttered an ear-piercing shriek and yelled, 'Snake! Snake!' We had disturbed a Great Western Brown coiled up under her chair.

All hell broke loose. Penny shot off through the gate and down the airstrip, the dogs were barking and trying to get into the room, as I was trying to shepherd the other two girls out, while yelling for Robbie and Rat to come with a gun. They came running with rifles. All of the noise and sudden activity must have frightened the snake, because it slithered out from under the chair and down through a small hole in the wall between the classroom and the food storeroom. Not a healthy place to be if you happen to be a poisonous snake.

Robbie and Rat tracked it back around into the storeroom and began gingerly lifting hessian bags of potatoes and rolling heavy drums of flour out of the way. They eventually forced it into a corner and shot its head off. John came out holding the snake up by the tail. Measured, the snake (minus its head) was 2.2 metres long. No amount of cajoling or threatening would entice Penny back into the classroom that day, so I let it slide and gave the kids the rest of the day off. If that sounds extremely lenient, it wasn't — those kids were genuinely terrified and would have been distracted and nervous all day, wondering if there were any more snakes around.

The only other reasons for suspending school lessons were the advent of visitors, including the Flying Doctor, and the arrival of the mail plane each week. These occurrences demanded at least a two-hour recess.

Visitors

One Wednesday when the FD arrived for his fortnightly clinic in the station's office, he had someone else with him. The stranger was a tall, blonde German Time/Life Magazine photographer, doing a story on *A Day in the Life of the Flying Doctor*. We turned on quite a show. My boss, Robbie, had just had a major fall from his horse (which we think shied at a snake or a goanna). He was covered in blood, needed a few stitches and a couple of injections. The photographer went crazy. I think he thought it was all turned on purely for his benefit. When it was my turn to see him, the FD said I needed a tetanus shot after some nasty scratches I had sustained from rusted barbed wire. In consultation with the photographer, he decided to give the injection to me standing under the wing of the Flying Doctor's plane — something he would ordinarily never do. Again, it made the photographer very happy. Never did see the story, of course.

The mail plane's arrival was much anticipated. Sometimes I used to send the girls a card or letter each, just so they would have something come in the mail for them and they would be very excited. I usually wrote messages like, 'Tracy, you have worked very hard at your school work this week. Well done!'

A gold star or a stamp on the back of the hand might have done, but would never have had such an impact on the kids. Their lessons from Brisbane came by post with about a four-week turnaround between completed lessons and new lessons. There were also library books, which the girls loved receiving. The mail would arrive in heavy locked canvas mailbags.

During the wet season there are few deliveries of mail because even the all-weather strip may be partially inundated. One year, the pilot simply dropped the mailbags from the plane, missed the strip and landed them in the raging green river. The bags were never recovered, and so that practice was forbidden from then onwards. We also shopped mostly from catalogues, with our cheque books, in those pre-credit-card days. Half of the time, I think we just ordered things for the pleasure of receiving them in the mail. Personal mail can be very precious to those living in isolated areas. This may be less so now, with the advent of computers, satellite dishes, Skype and email which have all caused the world to shrink. There is a less wonderful sense of anticipation than existed in those early days. Out on their fishing boat in the Gulf, however, my sister even now just loves receiving cards and letters in the mail. Theirs arrives about once a month by barge, not so very different from my days in the Gulf.

The Gregory Races and Race Ball

The most wonderful gifts visitors could bring were fresh fruit or vegetables, and news of the outside world. The newspapers we received were always at least a week or two old, but the news was fresh as far as we were concerned. There was always a queue of people waiting, but the boss was always the first to read it, then so on down the pecking order.

The greatest influx of visitors occurs on the May Day weekend, when the races are also held. There is no school over the long weekend, and it is not only the children who are excited. Following the races there is also the Annual Gregory Race Ball. This was one occasion when it was great being one of only several single girls in more than a hundred square kilometres — I never had the chance to sit down all night. I would just finish one dance and an almost unrecognisable ringer with slicked back, freshly washed hair, in dress shirt and trousers or fresh jeans would claim me for the next! Long dresses and suits or neat clean clothes for the men were *de rigeur*. Those who were not inclined to dance, spent most of the evening at the makeshift bar in the back yard of the hall. Most of the men were enthusiastic if improvising dancers. Friends of the McDowall family from Mt Isa or Townsville visited a few times that year, to hunt feral pigs, fish, camp, or in May to attend the Gregory Races, and the Gregory Canoe Race.

The Canoe Race is famous throughout Australia as one of the best courses on offer and runs for 43 kilometres. It began in 1976 with just 18 participants and has grown to over 100 kayakers and hundreds more spectators. There are also some spectacularly untouched sections of the Gregory River which are perfect for spectators and competitors alike for camping. The Canoe Race has been cancelled only three times since its inception, and that was because flooding had changed the flow of the river in some sections and made other sections too dangerous to navigate. The river is different each year, depending entirely on the way the wet season and volume of the natural springs cause changes in the flow. I have heard that in later years the river has sometimes ceased to flow at all because of the springs drying up.

The Gregory Races themselves involve more than just a few horse races. There are also some rodeo-style competitions such as the bull ride, barrel races, flag races, camp-drafting and calf roping (cutting a calf out of a small mob of cattle and either roping it or directing it into a pen from horseback). These races showcase the most important skills of the ringers, black and white. For the ladies, there were also a couple of novelty events such as the Broom Throw (I came second!) and Rolling-Pin Throw. The children have some riding events and other fun events such as the eternally-favourite sack race and egg and spoon race. Some of the children aged six to twelve rode as well as, if not better than, some of the adults and usually had no fear at all. Half of the activities on the day involve alcohol, but visitors attracted for the weekend come mostly for the fun and spectacle.

One of the activities I enjoyed most was a night picnic on the Gregory's bank near the old bridge. The 'local' ringers, governesses and the odd jillaroo, all brought food and drink, settled down on the bank and then swam in the dark waters of the river for a couple of hours by moonlight and starlight. It was a lot of fun, and one of my favourite memories of my time in the Gulf. The temperature of the water was just perfect for swimming and we gave no thought to freshwater crocs or sawfish. With the moonlight on the water, it was also very beautiful. It was another opportunity to get to know other young people in the district. Of course, there were a lot more young men than young women, but the odds were not at all bad from my point of view. Some of the guys opted to skinny dip, but others, like me, were too shy.

As for me, it was the first time I ever tasted rum. One of the ringers gave me a can of Coke and said, 'Here, drink half of this.' I did so, and he filled it to the brim with rum. That was the closest I have ever come to being sick from alcohol — the euphemistically called 'technicolour yawn'. If I catch so much as a whiff of rum now, all these years later, it instantly sends me back there. The men and quite a few of the 'rougher' women, were heavy drinkers. In fact, some of them drank most of the money they earned.

Once in a while, the two governesses from Punjab Station would come down to Gregory on a Friday or Saturday night and it was always fun when they were there. We even organised to go camping at the Twenty-Mile for a weekend. The Twenty-Mile was a gorgeous, untouched section of river with a small island in the middle, a narrow but deceptively deep tributary on one side and the main body of the river on the other. For some reason that I can't remember, we had the bright idea of driving Sara's car onto the island. It bogged up to the hubcaps. Jackie and I pushed and Sara drove. Jackie was 'built like a brick dunny' and lifted the back of the car up as I pushed. Eventually we succeeded, but were faced with the problem of getting it back to the mainland. Oh well, we would cross that tributary when we came to it. We built a fire, laid out our swags and set to catching some dinner. Sara was our fisherman extraordinaire and caught four sleepy cod. It was the best fish I have ever eaten, although we were a bit puzzled by the small, thin wiggling bits that popped out as Sara gutted them (my boss later told me that at certain times of the year, sleepy cod have worms). A bottle of Mateus Rosé cooled in the river just off the bank and washed down our meal.

Jackie had brought her guitar and I my mandolin. After a shaky beginning, the more wine we drank, the better we sounded. There was plenty of corned meat in case we failed to catch any fish. I hooked a freshwater tortoise and it made off with one of our two fishhooks, making Sara's fishing prowess even more impressive.

It was wonderful to be able to vent to others who knew what each of us was talking about. We had small gripes, but were basically happy in our jobs. All three of us appreciated the fact that one never knew what would happen from one day to the next, which made every day a unique adventure.

I never really thought about marrying a local although there was plenty of choice. I loved my time in the Outback, but had no ambition to live out my life there. Being young, it was an adventure, and all adventures come to an end sooner or later. There were other things I wanted to do with my life that did not include flies and dust.

Mum wearing her bridal gown modelled after the Disney princess gowns

My grandmothers celebrating at my parents' wedding

Chubby, afro-haired Susan

My great-grandparents, Mum, Dad, and Susan

Richard with Tommy the cat that adopted us

Susan's first day of school

Our house for about the first ten years of my life

Susan and Sandra on Nellie

Little Bo Peep (Susan) and Alice In Wonderland (Sandra)

off to Sunday School

Mum and the three of us, c.1968

Dad smoking his pipe on the back steps

*Susan, uncle Ian and aunt Rhonda, Mum,
at the opening of my first art exhibition*

*My parents' wedding day, Mum
wearing my family's Brides' Brooch*

Penny, Bronwyn and Tracy McDowall

Collage of some of my artwork

One of my English classes in Osaka - six kids and a rabbit

Susan working on the Information Desk at David Jones Department Store

Executive Secretary for QJCCI and AJSQ

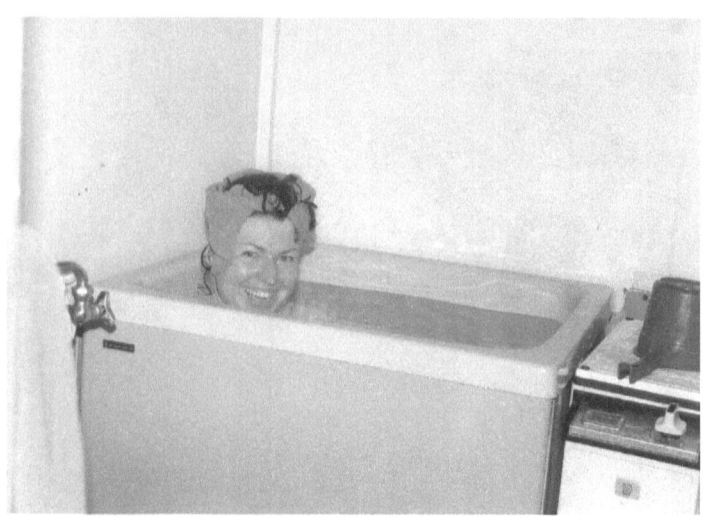
Susan in a Japanese bath

My university graduation

Richard's 40th birthday

a toast to Dad where we scattered his ashes

Mum and my stepfather, Mel

silent camel trek into the desert outside Alice Springs

My current flatmate Thomas

my new boyfriend, just a joke, Dad

Brisbane City Hall today.

Lawn Hill and Riversleigh Station Forays

Twice during the year, when some of the visitors from Mt Isa came up, we decided to visit Lawn Hill and Riversleigh, which were both working cattle stations in the area. (I use 'in the area' loosely to indicate that they were within a five-hour drive from Planet and Gregory). We left in a convoy of three four-wheel drive vehicles. There was also a journalist from Rockhampton, and unfortunately for him, he had to take a place sitting in the tray-back of one of the vehicles — he was pale, and redheaded, and burned to lobster redness, although at one point he took refuge under a blanket. A photograph he took of Tina Dorrington and me together with the two dogs the previous year, is the only photograph I have left from this period in my life, as I lost the remainder of them and some of my books to an outbuilding fire on Gregory Downs.

At that time, dinosaur skeletal remains had not been discovered on Riversleigh and there were few visitors to the property. Des and Desley, the Managers, generously allowed us the run of the place for a day after laying on a spread of homemade scones, fruitcake and strong tea. I was surprised to be able to pick up Aboriginal stone tools, just lying on the ground. Des had also told us about the 'ringing rocks'. These were large tufa formations balanced on top of one another with dozens of runnels down each side. If we gathered stones and tapped on the rock formations, we were astonished to find that they pealed like bells.

We continued on to Lawn Hill the next day and stopped to ask permission to camp there from Mr Maia, the Brazilian owner. He later sold the property to CRA Exploration as enormous zinc deposits were discovered there. In 1984, 12,000 hectares of the Lawn Hill property was gazetted as a national park — Boodjamulla National Park, land of the Waanyi people for an estimated 17,000 years. The Waanyi people only used the place for celebratory or ceremonial purposes. They believe that if the water is tampered with, or polluted, the Rainbow Serpent will leave and take away the water with it. There is a pristine series of three gorges, with a cave gallery of Aboriginal art above the end of the third gorge, which could be reached by kayak as long as there were two people to haul it up the steeply stacked rocks to the next gorge. The gorges are part of the Constance Range, laid down as sedimentary rock some 560 million years ago.

The water was a deep dark green and the depth at that time had not been plumbed. I guessed there would be freshwater crocodiles as well as plenty of fish and freshwater tortoises in the depths. Swimming in the lowest gorge, we discovered there was also an abundance of leeches in the surrounding rainforest and water. Still, it was great; sitting at the base of the waterfall on a rocky ledge, being pummelled by the wide cascade of water. Some of our group kayaked up to the end of the first gorge, and climbed with the kayaks up the rocks into the second and third gorges, which involved climbing up unbelievable piles of orange, brown and red rocks. They reported back on what they had seen in the Aboriginal cave gallery at the top of the third gorge. The men said that they had seen some true Aboriginal art that had been inside the low overhanging rocks that formed a shallow cave. My guess is that at least until that point, very few non-Indigenous people had seen the paintings. Some may have been painted fairly recently, and some may have been a thousand years or more in age.

There was an enormous colony of flying foxes roosting in the cabbage palms and eucalypts surrounding us, stirring after being asleep during the day. The sunset was almost obscured by dark screaming clouds of them. There were other animals we could hear scurrying around on the floor of the rainforest by the lapping water's edge, as though the cries of the flying foxes had acted as an alarm clock for them. We had a delightful three days there, camping, swimming, fishing, relaxing and exploring, without other people to annoy or disturb us.

The north-west's first acknowledged bushranger died on Lawn Hill in a shoot-out in 1889, thus ending the brief career of part-Aboriginal stockman, Joe Flick. Flick had fallen in love with an Aboriginal girl who was working at the Brook Wayside Inn on the property near the coach route. She ended their relationship and Flick flew into a rage against her employers, blaming them for her change of heart, and attacked them. When police arrived, he seemed to find that the mounts of the police made easier targets than the police themselves and shot several police horses.

He barricaded himself in the formally-decorated dining room at Lawn Hill homestead. The police surrounded him and kept watch on the dining room all through that rainy night. When they approached and searched the dining and surrounding rooms following a miserable sunrise, it was empty. Flick had escaped during the storm, and had climbed down the treacherous cliffs in front of the homestead, which had been built to take maximum advantage of the view across the wild valley. Flick was again bailed up, confronted. He shot several police before he himself was shot dead.

Now, I believe access to both Riversleigh and Lawn Hill is limited by permits, and there are ablution blocks for tourists. I don't think I would like to visit Lawn Hill again now — it wouldn't be the same. I would, however, love to go and see the dinosaur digs on Riversleigh and have placed it on my 'to do' list. Trips like our weekend forays into the surrounding country were rare and wonderful. Not having a car myself, I was limited in where I could go, but being given permission to go as part of a group was always very enjoyable. Sometimes if a trip was considered important enough, or if I had earned enough 'Brownie Points' with the boss, I would merit some time off.

The Business End of Gregory Downs

When all was said and done, Gregory, like all the other stations in the district, was a working cattle station. At some time in the past, a failed attempt had been made to turn Gregory Downs into a 'dude ranch'. I had seen a handsome red and silver roan gelding, half covered in mud, in the paddock with the night horses. Night horses are the ones kept in a paddock close to the homestead to round up the working horses needed for mustering and drafting work. I asked my boss Robbie about him. I asked if I could ride him. John's laughing reply was, 'Ha, if you can catch him, you can ride him.' Since all hands were needed for musters, I figured I needed a mount I could feel comfortable with rather than a different horse each time.

One afternoon during our rest time, I grabbed a carrot and a bridle (how naïve!) and let myself into the paddock. The roan was standing by himself chewing at some dry grass. I talked to him softly and held out the carrot, which he sniffed, then accepted. He dropped his head down as though giving me permission to slip on the bridle. I couldn't believe it had been so easy — this was a horse that had not been ridden in at least five years. He resisted at first, but then let me lead him to one of the house yards.

He was in terrible condition. His mane and tail had never been trimmed, and were full of three-centimetre *ngurra* burrs. These burrs are oval and covered with sharp spikes which end in needle-like little hooks. His coat was matted, he could hardly see because of the length of his forelock, and he was decidedly on the thin side. When I examined his teeth, I could see he was quite old as most of his teeth were worn down almost to the gums. This is a method usually used to estimate the age of a horse. I do not wish to give the impression that I am an expert, I can only tell the difference between 'young' and 'old'.

Over the best part of three afternoons of hard work, I teased out all of the burrs, and trimmed his mane, tail and silver forelock. I gave him grain, molasses, chaff and some of the chook food to eat and he wolfed it down as though he hadn't eaten for weeks. Next I washed him down and shampooed him. While I curry-combed his coat, he put his head on my shoulder and went to sleep. Now that was one relaxed horse! He came up beautifully — a rich red and shiny silver roan. He was 17 hands high at the withers and taller than any other horse I had ever ridden. One hand is equal to ten centimetres. Most horses for riding are in the 12 to 15 hands range. His fetlocks were heavily feathered, which, together with his size, may have pointed to some Clydesdale in his pedigree. Given that he was quite an old horse, he would not be a serious ride, but more of a pet.

I didn't know the horse's name, so I asked Robbie how I could find out. Together we looked through the old leather-bound stock books which contain records of all horses bought and sold by the Gregory's owners. We found out that his name was Larrikin, meaning 'cheeky, but good natured'. Because of his habit of throwing some riders, he was deemed unsuitable as a mount for the dude ranch that was earlier trialled, and so was simply left in a paddock to his own devices. That had been almost five years before. So at last, he had a name. The ringers, however, in recognition of his initial poor condition — his ribs were all visible when I first brought him in, nicknamed him Bony Roany. (Nicknames are very important in the Outback, and nearly everyone has one.) On the new diet regime I devised, Larrikin soon began to look sleek and fit, and after several shampoos and lots of brushing, his coat shone with good health. No other horses on the property were treated like this. Usually, they were given hay and feed, and water, locked in rough wooden-railed yards overnight, but left out when it rained, unless their paddocks flooded, at which attempts were made to move them to higher ground. None of them was washed, brushed or cossetted as I did with Larrikin.

The stock book also revealed that he was six months younger than I and that his working days were well and truly behind him. At 19, he was pretty old for a horse, although I have heard of a horse that lived to the age of 33. I was given another, much younger mount, an Australian Quarterhorse-cross for mustering duties and I mostly only rode Larrikin for pleasure and to give us both a little light exercise. He used to follow me around like a dog whenever I went to feed the pigs and chickens and let him out of his yard. I have never known a horse with a sweeter disposition. Horses are no different than any other animal — they respond well to gentleness and kindness.

The travelling district farrier visited us one afternoon while I was grooming Larrikin and said, 'I know this horse! I reshod him about six or seven years ago. I could do anything I wanted with him.' He proceeded to demonstrate by lifting each of the horse's hooves in turn, then ducking under his belly, something that most horses dislike intensely. Larrikin just stood there and calmly accepted everything the farrier demonstrated on him. I am sure I could have put all three children on his back at once and that he would have behaved perfectly, but the girls were quite indifferent to him.

Running cattle is not a case of simply turning them out into a pasture and rounding them up after a year or so to truck them off to the sale yards. There is a schedule of things that need doing at different times of the year. When the cattle are mustered for the first muster of the year, they are separated into calves and yearlings, cows, heifers (young cows of breeding age that had not yet been bred), bulls and steers (castrated males). The calves are moved up a race of metal tubing and old rubber truck tyres enable the calf to be thrown on its side without being injured or having to be roped. After being caught in the calf cradle, everything happens at once, the male calves are castrated with razor-sharp knives, and all the calves are earmarked, tagged and branded — all with three or four ringers working together at the various tasks. Understandably, the calves have something to bellow about as they come out of the calf cradle and down the other side of the race.

Any males not wanted for breeding are castrated. Any cows not wanted for breeding are spayed by a vet (the ovaries are removed), in conditions far from ideal. Spaying and castrating also make the cattle put on weight, so they will fetch a better price at market and also ensure that less desirable cattle do not breed.

During the year, the cattle are dipped in pesticides to kill off any ticks on them. It means moving them up a crush one after the other, then down into a bath of pesticide so that they have to swim to the end and climb out. As well as this, all of the cattle are 'drenched'. Drenching involves a long tube with a trigger mechanism, containing medication which is to protect the cattle from botulism and brucellosis. These things are usually done in groups over a week or more as it would be impossible to process several thousand head of cattle all at once. The ringers and bosses work incredibly hard at these tasks and need to be fit and strong to accomplish them.

In the evening after a day of castrating the male calves, there is usually a barbeque. Thankfully, when I was offered 'prairie oysters', I declined, much to the disappointment of the ringers who sat around grinning, waiting for it to dawn on me what they really were. I disappointed them by not falling for the trick. I will bet that is one kind of oyster that nobody chews. I had also been offered an 'emu apple' from a bush in a paddock we were riding through on the same day. I tried it and couldn't get the horrible taste out of my mouth. They were actually quinine berries. The boss and the ringers loved playing tricks like that on me, and would laugh uproariously if I fell for one. Never mind, I loved playing tricks on them too.

The breeding bulls were given special attention and were looked over carefully whenever they were brought in. It was not unusual to see one of the heavyweight breeder bulls standing in the river during the heat of the day, cooling his testicles. Bull testicles look like two fat pork sausages. When selecting breeding bulls, the circumference of the bull's testicles is measured. The larger the circumference, the better or more fertile the bull, according to animal husbandry research.

Mustering these days is assisted by helicopter and four-wheel drives, as well as riders on horseback accompanied by trained cattle dogs, that can often break through scrubby areas that the vehicles cannot, to round up strays and breakaways. The muster can take anywhere from three days to a week, necessitating all hands not needed at the homestead to be out in 'camp'. The work was hot, dry and dusty, but I loved the atmosphere around the fire at night as unsettled dust clouds drifted around the camp, my behind and thighs aching, especially after the first day. My arms would be stiff and throbbing and I would sink into sleep as soon as I lay down in the swag, to the accompaniment of the gentle murmur of the men's voices, the lowing of cattle, and the odd crackle from the dying fire. It was wonderful to fall asleep from sheer physical weariness, since I have always been a poor sleeper. I wasn't really needed at other times because I had only my year on Planet Downs as experience in active cattle mustering, but looked upon it as a privilege to be there. Up again before first light, just an apricot glow below the horizon, for a quick breakfast of damper, meat and tea. There was the soft jingle of bridles as the horses were saddled, then out into the paddocks once more just as the sun rose, wondering if I would ever walk properly again. Although I had grown up around horses, the kind of riding required by ten hours and more in the saddle each day was far more rigorous than I was used to. Many older men in the Outback are permanently bowlegged from a lifetime in the saddle.

The Night Before

When helicopters were used in a muster, it was common for the pilot to stay with the family at the end of each day, eat with them and be billeted in the house rather than in the men's quarters. On one such night, Rat was hinting that I was keen on the chopper pilot, whom I had only just met. I was so embarrassed, that I said to Rat, 'How would you like me to tip this bowl of custard on your head?'

'You wouldn't.'

I did. Rather than being angry or shocked, the whole family roared with laughter as Rat sat mutely at the table with creamy yellow custard dripping from his black beard. In retaliation, Rat grabbed the two-litre water jug from the middle of the table, pushed me down on the linoleum floor and poured the entire contents over me. For Rat and me, it was the start of a beautiful relationship: one of us would play a practical joke on the other, and it would escalate with each of us trying to outdo the other one. Strictly nothing harmful or malicious — that was the unwritten rule. We made our own fun.

As Rat was head stockman, he was given the head stockman's cottage, even though he wasn't married. I thought long and hard about how I could booby-trap his cottage from front door to back door. Starting with the front door, I syruped all the door handles and light switches, sprinkled talcum powder on the polished wooden floor, hid all of the light bulbs in the refrigerator, soaped his toothbrush, put cling film under the black toilet seat, and Vegemite on it. From there I went to the bedroom: cornflakes in the pillowcase, short-sheeted the bed, placed a peeled, overripe banana in the bottom of the bed, unpaired all of his socks and paired them up oddly (he wore odd socks for almost a month and since he frequently wore jeans or riding pants that were too short, they were very obvious!) I put rice in his boots and tied all of the lace-ups together. Little tricks that would be found over time, rather than all at once. Mind you, I also did the cleaning up once he had discovered all of my tricks, which I thought was only fair!

By far my greatest stroke of genius was to stitch closed the legs of all of his underpants. The kids tipped him off, 'Uncle Rat, Uncle Rat, Miss K has been in your house!' He entered the cottage very slowly and warily while I maintained an expression of studied innocence.

The main house had an ablution block behind it with gas hot water, which Rat also used, rather than light up the 'donkey' boiler at the back of his cottage each night. As he headed for the shower with his clean clothes over his arm that evening, I said to Veronica, 'Watch this, it should be great.' Fifteen minutes later, Rat came out of the shower, wearing his clothes, and never said a word about the stitches in his underpants or his odd socks. What a letdown! I had expected histrionics and fireworks. We both knew it was his move next in our funny version of the funniest available board game.

I went away camping again with a couple of other governesses one weekend and had left a pair of my jeans on the clothesline. When I brought them in on my return, I found large clumsy stitches in the legs, which I thought was very tame. He did retaliate though, the next afternoon after school, he walked into the classroom where I was preparing the next day's lessons, and without a word, picked me up, threw me over his shoulder, walked the hundred metres or so down to the bridge ... and threw me into the river! The kids were laughing so hard they were rolling around, with tears in their eyes. We were the entertainment. When I left Gregory Downs almost a year later, Rat put his arm around my shoulder and said, 'You know, I'm going to miss you.'

The One Mile

As the May school holidays drew near, the kids were sick of me and I of them. I needed to get away for a bit, for my sake and theirs, so I asked my boss, Robbie, if I could go camping down at the One Mile, which was a clear stretch of riverbank, not far from the end of the closer of the two plane runways. He asked how long I was wanting to camp. I hadn't really thought about that part, so I blurted out, 'the whole two weeks'.

'What will you do for food for that long?'

'I'll take what I need with me, and can come back for more at the end of the first week,' I replied. 'Besides, I will want to collect my mail.'

One of the ringers gave me a lift to the area a little past the runway's end, beyond the tree line. I had a swag, a two-man tent, and for provisions: flour, rice, sugar, coffee, a large piece of cake and another piece of corned beef, as well as a hand line and several fishhooks. I had a good selection of books and a small radio with which I could pick up the ABC broadcast via Mt Isa. Thinking I could rig a cool box by placing the meat in a small lidded white bucket, placing it in the river with a broken branch connecting it to the bank for the purpose of weighing it down. I didn't know ants could get through plastic — they used the branch as though it was a purpose-made bridge! That was the end of my meat supply. Rather than admit defeat, I had damper for almost every meal except for the solitary black bream I caught.

One day when I was sitting ah, unclothed in the midday heat, in the shallow water reading a book, I heard a '*phut, phut*' kind of sound, and looked up just in time to see two kayakers in training, gliding past. 'This was supposed to be the geographic centre of Nowhere,' I fumed. I sprang up, dropped the book in the water and dashed behind a tree but I had been seen.

'Hello there!'

That was my first and last skinny dip there.

In the afternoons, I would collect dried cowpats from the plentiful supply in the surrounding bush for the fire each night. Dried cow dung on a fire will help repel mosquitoes, and it actually has quite a pleasant scent, unlike the way it smells fresh when you step in it. On that first night, I had built myself a small fire in a scooped out area of sand, and was listening to the radio. Suddenly, I heard dingoes not too far away. Then there was a crash, and 'Shut up you bloody idiot, she'll know it's us.'

'You can come and sit by the fire for a while, boys, and then you have to go.'

The ringers, both in their early twenties, had been drinking and had decided at the pub that Friday evening that it would be great fun to sneak through the bush and scare the governess at her riverbank camp. We talked about how they had each come to be on Gregory Downs, which I found really interesting. I doubt that many other people had expressed an interest in their stories before that time. The boys became genuinely nostalgic over the circumstances that had led our paths to cross.

That first night on my own was wonderful. I heard sleepy cattle nearby, curlews, and plains turkeys — bustards, but knew they wouldn't harm me. There were thousands of stars in the moonless bowl overhead, shedding nearly enough light to read by. I could almost feel the weight of them pressing down around me. There was an elderly bush poet from Georgetown (hours away nearer the coast), on the ABC radio, and I really enjoyed listening to his poetry. I later wrote to him and we shared a brief correspondence for a few months.

At the end of the first week, I walked all the way back to the homestead, greeted the family and collected mail and some fresh supplies. Clearly, I would only be able to take enough meat for one or two days, without any kind of refrigeration. That must have been a constant problem for the earliest settlers there, which, I'm guessing, would be why they and we had so much salted meat.

The three kids greeted me enthusiastically and asked about my camp. I was glad to see them, and have a cup of tea with Veronica before I left to walk back again. The second week was uneventful, and by the end of that time, I had had enough of my own company to last me through the coming school term. When I returned, the kids hugged me as though they hadn't seen me for months. I am sure the break did all of us some good. Robbie thought it was weird for a woman to want to camp alone in the bush, and shook his head in amusement.

Irishman with a Machete

Early one afternoon in the classroom, we heard a ruckus with dogs barking and men yelling, down near the river bank. The kids wanted desperately to see what all the excitement was about, so I gave them permission to join the men, and scrambled down the river bank in their wake.

Two of the Indigenous stockmen had caught a water python nearly three and a half metres long. The other stockmen were standing around looking at it, as two of them stretched it out to its full muscular length.

'You fellas going to eat it?' one of them asked.

'Nah, don't like snake,' said Albert. 'Too many bones.'

Rat offered the idea of forcing the muscular, writhing snake into a large, brown hessian potato sack, and taking it across the river to the pub. At that time, the publicans were Phil and Cathy Kerlin. Phil was Irish, and terrified of snakes. The ringers let the python loose on the floor of the bar. Pandemonium erupted! Phil jumped up on the bar, his face white. While brandishing a machete, he was using some four-letter words I had never heard before. There were dogs, tourists, ringers — everyone shouting at once. The poor, harmless snake was terrified and made a quick getaway out the side door into the scrub, and no doubt, back to the nearby river. The boys thought it was a great joke, and it took a while for Phil to live down his reaction. As part of the joke, the boys would enter the bar and yell, 'Snake!' every time they went there over the ensuing months, until Phil no longer reacted to their teasing.

Sometimes it was categorically necessary to pep things up a little at the pub, so jokes like 'the Great Snake Escape' not only provided fodder for conversation long after the event, but also entered the annals of local history. Friday nights while we were relaxing could be a bit dull, sitting talking to the same people each week. After I'd had a drink or two which was enough for me, I would go behind the bar and help Phil serve, just to alleviate the encroaching boredom. At other times I would join Cathy in the pub's kitchen to peel vegetables. Cathy had been the matron at the three-bed Burketown cottage hospital for many years, and always had some interesting stories to tell. It wasn't uncommon for me to be the only female customer, unless the Punjab girls had made the long drive down, in which case we tended to congregate together and share teaching stories, tricks and ideas for improving our performance in the classroom.

Cathy told me a story about a snakebite victim, which may or may not have been true, but it had a ring of truth about it. A male tourist visiting the Gregory district was bitten by a taipan through his canvas shoe. His foot and leg were bandaged tightly in an attempt to limit the spread of the poison and he was bedded down in the back of a Hilux as a makeshift ambulance, then speedily driven the 120 kms over rough, unsurfaced road to the little three-bed Burketown Hospital. The driver radioed ahead to the hospital that he was bringing in a snakebite victim. The patient was treated immediately upon arrival, and after days of hovering between life and death from a bite that was almost always fatal, he recovered. As he was dressing to leave the hospital some days later, he dropped dead. It was found that one of the snake's hollow fangs had broken off in the wall of his canvas shoe. There was enough of the extremely potent venom remaining on the embedded fang to penetrate his skin and kill him.

One Friday night, a young ringer named Rick from one of the outlying stations was at the bar with an assortment of other ringers, managers and visitors. He complained of pain in a rotten front tooth and he had one black tooth mid-smile. The other ringers who were drinking at the pub that night conferred and decided it was time for a little DIY dentistry. They made sure Rick was good and drunk, then knocked the front tooth out with a small hammer borrowed from someone's toolbox. Rick was so drunk that he felt no pain, fell asleep, and woke up the following morning with a massive hangover but with the troublesome tooth gone. Problem solved.

On a slow Saturday afternoon at the pub, I borrowed a pair of scissors and cut one of the ringer's hair in the front yard at his request, even though I protested that I had never done it before. Soon there was a queue. One of my victims, Silas, our Latvian grader driver, kept asking me to take more and more off. So I obliged, not really sure how much he would consider 'enough'. He was almost bald by the time I finished with him. He wore a hat for about two months, even indoors and in the face of custom, and never asked me to cut his hair again. I have to admit, though, that the more of the men's hair I cut, the better the outcome. Practice makes perfect. Another young ringer, Trevor, known to all and sundry as 'Prickly Bush' because of his longish crew cut, was another of my 'customers', only he was a lot fussier than the others. I guess I can now add 'barber' to my list of skills and accomplishments.

If I went anywhere with the boys on a winter night, there was always a fight over who had to drive. It was not desirable, but more of a booby prize. The rest of us would throw a mattress in the back of the Hilux, a few blankets, and would squeeze into the back, becoming drunk on the magnificent spectacle of the stars spread out by their millions high above us. With no ambient light from houses or streetlights, it was pitch dark and the stars stood out with a clarity I have never seen anywhere else. Being on a flat plain, the sky looked like a perfect, uninterrupted black hemisphere: the sight was awesome, and sometimes we could also see tiny satellites which showed as green dots tracking across the sky.

Little did I know, that a situation would soon present itself when I was never more appreciative of even faint starlight.

The Flat Tyre

Veronica, the three children and I had left before daybreak for a quick trip into Mt Isa which was six hours each way. On the way back we called in at the property where Robbie's other brother was manager, a couple of hours' drive from Gregory Downs. An hour and a half's drive or so from Gregory, there was a tremendous bang as the rear right tyre suddenly blew. Veronica swore, coasted to a stop, and opened the door of the station wagon. She opened the rear to remove the toolbox and jack. There *was* a spare tyre, and there *was* a jack, but for some reason known only to himself, Robbie had removed the toolbox from the rear of the station wagon and not replaced it.

Veronica sat in the dirt, legs splayed out, trying to get the wheel nuts off with the only tool in the vehicle: a bottle opener. John was called by quite a few colourful epithets, and his parentage questioned as she poked and prodded the wheel nuts to no avail. We were approximately fourteen kilometres on a rough dirt road from the homestead, and it was just on dusk. We had no phone or radio to contact the homestead (something it is very wise to have on one at all times). We briefly discussed who should go for help. Obviously, Veronica should stay with the children, which left me.

Determined to be brave, and although I was quite scared at the thought of a startled bull attacking me, or worse, I said I would walk to the homestead and send Robbie to fetch his family, WITH the toolbox.

I had a small torch, which died after about 100 metres, and beyond that, could only rely on starlight, as there was no moon. Walking in the middle of the road, I clapped my hands, sang songs, and recited as many as I could remember of the Periodic Table of the Elements, limericks and other fragments of poetry, trying to warn any animals in my way, to move. I encountered four Droughtmaster cattle sleeping in the middle of the road. I also frightened a pair of bustards in the soft bulldust right beside the road in the rustling grass, which was taller than I. They almost scared me to death as they suddenly shrieked in alarm and broke cover. There were many other noises which I could not identify and had no desire to do so.

I made it to the sleeping pub, which was in darkness when I arrived, and sighed with relief that I had less than two kilometres to go to the homestead. By this time it was just after 1am. Dragging myself up the stairs, I walked into the main bedroom and roused Robbie, who was sound asleep, told him what had happened, and that he had to fetch his family, taking a toolbox if he knew what was good for him and if he even remotely wanted to consider being able to father more children! I asked him if he hadn't been worried when we didn't make it home by dinner time. 'No, I thought you must have stayed the night at my brother's place.' Had we done so, Veronica would have sent a message by the two-way to let him know not to expect us until the next morning.

'I, am going to bed. You can't miss them, they're on the road about twelve or fourteen kilometres back.'

Robbie dressed hastily and, grabbing a tool box from one of the sheds, opened the door to the Land Cruiser in one fluid movement. I crashed fully clothed on my bed and did not remember anything else until several hours past breakfast.

Veronica apparently tore strips off him for not checking with his brother on the two-way radio. They made it safely home by around 3.30 am, allowing time to actually change the tyre and settle Veronica down. I gave the kids the day off as they were feral from lack of sleep, and I doubted my ability to get through the full day, too. I went back to bed and slept until lunchtime and then felt human enough to help Veronica with some of the cooking for the family in the afternoon.

Thereafter, whenever Veronica, the kids and I went anywhere in the station wagon, she checked to make sure there were: a spare tyre, plenty of bottled water (whatever you think you'll need, double it), some dry biscuits, a good first aid kit, and a complete tool box — she no longer trusted Robbie to have returned everything he borrowed.

That would have to be one of the scariest experiences of my life. But still, there was nothing for it but to grit my teeth and go, or we could have been stuck by the side of the road anything from hours to days before someone came along and rescued us. By then we may have succumbed to dehydration and hunger.

Lack of preparedness in the Outback can kill you. Literally. I did not overstate the seriousness of the situation.

All Toyotas Aint Toyotas

Whenever a light plane came in to land, the pilot would fly low over the homestead and 'buzz' us to let us know he needed to use the landing strip. Then someone would jump into the old Toyota tray-back — so decrepit that it was kept only for the purpose of clearing the airstrip of cattle, kangaroos and any other miscellaneous life forms that had wandered onto it in the path of a plane. I asked for permission to do the job, but not having driven before, I had a few of the Toyota's foibles to acquaint myself with first.

The Toyota was a tray-back, and that's where the similarities to more recent models ended. The driver's side door was long gone, its absence outlined in various shades of rust. The bench seat, too, was gone, and in its place an upended flour drum draped in a hessian potato sack served the driver, with nothing for a passenger. Where there had once been a normal set of gears, it now jumped from first to third and the brakes didn't work. To stop, the driver had to change gears down to first and take their feet off the pedals, so that the gutsy little workhorse of a vehicle would coast to a stop (as long as they were not on an incline). Doing 360s on the airstrip in an anticlockwise fashion was therefore out of the question unless said driver was hell-bent on being flung out into the dust and gravel. It had no lights, but then planes only landed there during daylight hours — no problem. The horn only worked every second or third try, which was a bit of a disadvantage when the whole point was to scare animals off the strip. Still, it had a function in station life and was eminently suited for its single role. The manufacturers would have been ecstatic to know that virtually all of the original paint was intact.

It was the only station vehicle I was allowed to drive, as I had no licence at the time. One heavy, heat-hazed afternoon I decided to take it down to the river, across the rickety wooden bridge, up the other side past Snobs Hill, and on to the pub. Prickly Bush was hanging around outside the nearby cattle yard and I asked him if he wanted to come (I didn't mention I had zero driving skills). He replied that he needed some more smokes, shrugged his shoulders and jumped up on the back. I crept along very slowly, not sure how fast I was going because the speedometer didn't work either. We crawled over the absurdly-narrow bridge with about 30 centimetres to spare on either side, wobbled on past Snobs' Hill and approached the pub's fence. I couldn't stop in time and a part of the fence ended up bowed in where the truck finally came to rest. Prickly Bush jumped down, tweaked the brim of his old felt Stetson hat at me and said tersely that he would walk back. Sometimes, when I think of that old Toyota, I wonder what the manufacturers would have made of such a wreck of their handiwork, still soldiering on under conditions they never could have envisaged.

Two days later Prickly Bush gave notice. The stockmen only half-jokingly blamed me for giving him a real fright and scaring him into leaving. Seriously, my driving was not so bad, for someone who had no idea what they were doing.

Many years later, at the ripe old age of 30, I did sit the test for my licence and passed on my first attempt. Now, in my late fifties, I have never yet owned a car. In the Outback, I didn't need one, in Japan only the wealthy or those living in remote areas own cars, and the public transportation network is probably second to none in the world. I live so close to the city now that there is reasonable public transport and I cannot justify the expense of owning a car that would sit in the garage for most of the week. However, I have many times fantasised about owning a bright, bright yellow Audi. Chauffeur-driven, of course. Yellow, because people would see me coming and get out of my way, and Audi because I liked the TV commercials which emphasised luxury, precision engineering, and almost-orgasmic driving pleasure. Might be a bugger to get parts for if anything went wrong, because they would more than likely need to be imported. Funny thing — although you can see plenty of old Mercedes Benz, plenty of vintage Volkswagens and even Volvos, I am yet to see old-model Audis on the roads — either a very good or very bad sign regarding their longevity.

Last Call

At the close of my year on Gregory, the McDowall family decided to move to Cairns, as Robbie was keen to work in the Stock Squad in the Queensland Police Force. Sadly, I lost touch with the family and never heard what became of the three little girls. That was until, through the magic of Facebook some 40 years later, I saw their names. Thinking it unlikely there would be three other women with their names, I was able to contact them. They are all mums now with children of their own. Robbie went on to manage a number of other cattle stations.

The McDowalls agreed to drive me to Mt Isa, but after that, I would be on my own. On the way, we stopped in a nowhere place called Quamby. Quamby consisted of a railway siding, a pub and a black water tower on a high platform, the barest minimum to service a widely-scattered clientele. Incongruously, it also boasted a telephone booth. I contacted friends in Mt Isa and they offered to have me stay until I went back south to Brisbane.

We were in the middle of a grasshopper plague. Had I not *needed* to use that phone booth, nothing in the world could have induced me to enter it. Thanks to its bright fluorescent light, every grasshopper within a two hundred kilometre radius was trying to squeeze in there with me — they were going down inside my shirt, up the legs of my jeans, in my face, in my hair — everywhere! I was nearly hysterical by the time I stepped out of the booth. If you see anyone wearing one of the T-shirts sold at the pub that say, 'Where the Hell is Quamby?' I know. I've been there.

I stayed with Mark, the PCAP teacher, and his wife Jenny in Mt Isa for a few days, then bought train tickets to take me to Townsville and from there to Brisbane. Not having much money, I subsisted on sandwiches and the odd cup of coffee for the long trip home. I met a lovely man named Bruce on the train. He was a cane cutter from Mackay and was heading south to look for other work. He was very friendly, and taught me a couple of card games to while away the time. When we arrived in Brisbane, my mother wasn't expecting me, but I only had ten cents left as it was a weekend and I couldn't access my bank account (no ATMs back then). Bruce kindly gave me the money to call home, and offered to wait with me until my mother came to collect me. Where are the men like Bruce these days — the gentleman is quietly dying out in the savage face of Women's Liberation, Equality and Political Correctness. Men these days are not sure what they are expected to do — some of their gallantry such as opening doors for a lady is often rebuffed now. It must be very confusing for them. If a man offers to open a door for you, or offers you a seat — a woman shouldn't say no. He is making a concerted effort to act the way his mother taught him, and he knows that is the right thing to do. By not accepting, women are effectively saying, 'Leave me alone, I know what I'm doing and I don't need your help.' In saying yes, a woman is saying 'Thank you — your parents brought you up the right way and you have good manners.' With the emergence of a strong multicultural movement, it has become even more confusing.

My days of being a governess in the Outback were officially over. I was one of the last of a generation of 'governesses', they were soon to be called 'home supervisors' and have evolved to now being called 'home tutors', with a different, narrower job description. Now there are fewer home tutors and the children have satellite dishes, computers, Skype and a faster turn-around time by email for their lessons, as I discovered when I recently visited the School of the Air in Alice Springs. The new technologies are changing the way children are taught in the Outback. Seeing the computers and other learning aids Outback kids now had access to, brought unexpected tears to my eyes.

BRISBANE

Ah, Soo Desu Ka?

On my second day back in Brisbane, while perusing the 'Wanted' ads in the *Courier Mail*, I found a vacant position for a waitress in a Japanese restaurant. I knew absolutely nothing about working in a restaurant other than a few months' experience in a brasserie, but I had fed large groups of people, had been to Japan, and I could speak the language, things I thought would work in my favour. I called the number in the ad, and made a time for an interview for two-thirty the following afternoon in the city centre. The restaurant was in an old, two-storey wooden building on the corner of Creek and Queen Streets, where an office high-rise now stands.

I was competing with four other hopefuls and my resume wasn't much to look at at that stage of my life, but I sat there smiling, and answered every one of Mr Tsukamoto's English questions in Japanese. At the end, he said 'Aa, soo desu ka.' This can have a variety of meanings: everything from 'Oh, really,' to 'Is that so?' to a satisfied 'There now,' to a sarcastic 'Oh, yeah?' I wasn't quite sure which one he meant at first. After the interview, he sighed and said, 'You can have the job. Sit over there and wait while I interview the others.'

Sometimes just being in the right place at the right time (with the right language!) is enough.

Mr Tsukamoto told me I could start that night, and I was given a uniform — a coarsely-woven red and black mid-calf gown, superficially something like a kimono, except it had elasticised sleeves so that they wouldn't drag in the food as we were serving or cooking at the table, and a narrow tie around the waist instead of an *obi*. The length of the coarse red and black gowns revealed our calves. And we wore *tabi* socks in our *zoori* shoes. The uniform, just like a real *kimono*, had to be tied correctly — first over the heart and then to the right. Only corpses are dressed in the opposite way and Japanese patrons would certainly notice if they were tied incorrectly. It made me laugh when an Australian customer asked why Japanese women whose *obi* were mostly tied in the *taiko* (drum shape), were wearing parachutes with their *kimono*!

The restaurant, named *The Shoki*, had a cosy atmosphere with large, brightly-coloured waxed paper umbrellas softening some of the lights, wood and paper screens and freestanding bamboo screens delineating a number of private dining rooms; a bar, and two very large fish tanks. In Japanese mythology, *Shoki* was the god of the underworld and exorcism, and also the god worshipped to ward off illness and bad luck — an all-round good guy.

One tank held live lobsters and mud crabs for diners to choose, and the other held an assortment of tiny reef fish that Mr Tsukamoto had caught himself. As a joke, he named each of the little reef fish after one of the waitresses. One waitress who worked there, Etsuko, was quite plump and had a cheerful, round face. He named the blowfish after her. My fish was a delightful little mudskipper that would play in the bubbles from the filter at the back of the tank. The mudskipper would dive through the twin streams of bubbles, turn around and then do it again and again. It could keep up its play for ages before it tired and sank down to the sandy floor of the tank. It had bright and curious eyes and would often follow movement outside the tank.

That first night, I met the other staff properly, and one of the chefs said,

'You don't recognise me, do you?'

'You look a little familiar, but I'm sorry, no.'

'I'm Tommy Eldridge. We were at primary school together. My sister Jane and I came from Malaysia. You were the only one who was kind to us when we first arrived.'

Once he said that, I did remember him, although I had no recollection of being especially kind to them. We used to walk home from school together as far as their house, the five of us, including my brother and sister. Sometimes their mother would have tasty little Malaysian snacks waiting for us, and then Sandi, Richard and I would continue on to our home.

On my first night waitressing at *The Shoki*, I had the onerous task of carrying a 60-centimetre-long pine *sashimi* boat to a customer's table. The feature creature was a large lobster sitting prominently in the bow, cut in half behind the head, with its tail turned inside out and the raw meat diced neatly into two-centimetre pieces on top. To my horror, the front half was still moving and crept along the edge of the pine boat, touching my outstretched bare arm. I screamed in alarm and almost dropped Chef's artfully arranged lobster, oysters, fresh fish, prawns, scallops and crab legs all over the floor. The Japanese manager took me aside and with a scowl on his face and a menacing finger in mine, told me that I would be fired if I scared the patrons like that again. Not an auspicious first night on the job. It also brought home to me just *how* fresh Japanese patrons expected their seafood to be!

One of the features separating this restaurant from the other couple of Brisbane Japanese restaurants at the time was that certain meals patrons could order were cooked by their waitress at the table. Each table featured a gas bottle underneath and a gas burner above. After every lunch sitting, one or another of the waitresses was rostered to crawl under each table and change the gas bottles so that they wouldn't suddenly empty during a meal, leaving it half-cooked. It was a tedious and uncomfortable task, and one that none of us relished.

It took me a while to become adept at cooking in front of customers. We had to use *oohashi* — literally 'big chopsticks' — about 40 centimetres long. Once, I dropped half a crab in a man's lap.

'Oh, I'm so sorry!'

'No worries, love,' and he picked it up by one leg and tossed it into the cooking pot.

There was another occasion when I dropped a sliced, half an onion onto the table, and one man of the three couples at the table looked at me with disdain and said he expected a lot better. He went on to criticise my skills and was eventually told to shut up by two female customers at the table. Very embarrassing, but it took a reasonable amount of skill and practice to snare all the slices of a slippery, sliced onion-half simultaneously and place it in the pot as I had been taught.

The restaurant opened at 11.00 am for the lunch session, and closed at 2 pm. That left three hours before we prepared for the dinner sitting and reopened at 6 pm. Split shifts are probably the worst thing about working in hospitality. During those three hours, the other waitresses, the chefs and kitchenhands and I would select an inviting section of carpet, or line up several chairs and sleep for two to three hours.

The staff there were like family — we always ate dinner and lunch together after the customers had gone and it really was like being around the family table, with Mr Tsukamoto as the patriarch. I turned 21 while working there, and the boss generously told me I could choose anything from the menu for the whole staff for dinner which we usually ate around midnight or later. I chose *sukiyaki*, and he unexpectedly gave us two bottles of Dom Perignon champagne as well. It was a great twenty-first birthday party.

Tommy the chef and Meredith, one of the waitresses, were engaged and were due to be married. It was a real '*Shoki* family' affair — Mr Tsukamoto offered his silver Mercedes as the bridal car. Tommy's sister Jane was the bridesmaid, I sang and played guitar at the wedding, and we all chipped in for the wedding cake. They were married in the lovely brown and white Albert Street Uniting Church in Brisbane's city centre, and the reception was held in the yard of their little workers' cottage in Red Hill. Tommy's sister Jane wore a knee-length apricot dress. She was so nervous during the ceremony that I could actually see from my position behind her that her knees were shaking!

After around six months, I became the head waitress. That meant that I was ultimately in charge of the reservations book, the cash drawer and a number of miscellaneous duties above and beyond waitressing. The best part was that I was largely able to pick and choose which customers I served and had quite a few favourites.

I enjoyed cooking dishes such as *sukiyaki* and *mizutaki* at the table for customers, and as we had a large regular clientele, it came to feel like cooking for friends in my own home. It created a relaxed and friendly atmosphere and our diners really enjoyed the experience. For dishes cooked at table, the ingredients must be added in a specific order and at certain intervals so that the result is perfectly cooked. After I had left the restaurant, I actually did go to the home of two regular customers and cooked *sukiyaki* and other dishes for them. They told me they had not returned to the *Shoki* since I'd left, since it 'just wasn't the same any more'. I had always arranged it so that if I saw their names in the reservations diary, I would assign myself their table. The woman was an Emergency Room doctor and her fiancé was an anaesthesiologist.

One memorable night, I was reduced to very unprofessional tears. Everything that could possibly go wrong *did* go wrong. We had a party of six Italians booked for one of the private dining cubicles, separated from the neighbouring cubicles by freestanding bamboo screens. I slid open the door and stood aside for them to enter and be seated. The first disaster of the night occurred when one of the three ladies sat on her chair and went straight through it. The unattached seat had tilted and fallen through, which they tended to do unless they were set squarely on the timber frame. Her behind was on the floor and her legs were waving in the air. We had to tip the chair on its side in order to free her. The other two women and three men were all laughing at her. Once they were settled, I took their order and beat a hasty retreat. This incident made me nervous, a fact which probably contributed to the rest of the disasters of the night.

A man in the next cubicle rocked back on his chair and sent a bamboo screen crashing down on my Italians' table, bringing howls of protest from them. I rushed back in to right the screen and check on the people in the next cubicle. No major damage.

I brought the drinks order. The Italian group had all decided to try warm *sake* and declared that it was better than *grappa*. The problem with *sake*, particularly when it is warm, is that one can become tipsy very quickly. They were quite merry by the time their dinner orders were ready. They had ordered *Sukiyaki* on one burner and chicken *mizutaki* on the other, to be cooked by me and shared by all six of them. I brought in the tray of six lacquered bowls of soup, placed one on the table, and one more followed of its own volition, spilling the contents everywhere (I wondered briefly if anyone had ever calculated the surface area that volume of soup could cover). I hurriedly placed the others down and ran to get a cloth to mop up the spill and also a replacement bowl. One of the men ended up with a wet crotch. I offered to pay for the dry cleaning, but he just waved me away saying that it was of no consequence. I did not offer to help him mop it up.

Cooking two dishes at once is a little challenging, but I managed fairly well, with one ear on the steady stream of questions: How did I come to be working in a Japanese restaurant when I wasn't Japanese? Did I speak the language? Did I have a Japanese parent? Had I ever been there? Who taught me to cook Japanese food? And so on. Then, horrors — one of the two gas bottles ran out! I mentally cursed whomever was responsible that day for replacing them at lunch time and hadn't. I went out to the storeroom, fetched a new bottle and then had to crawl in amongst the moving forest of twelve human and 28 wooden legs to replace it. I kept telling my Italian customers that this normally never happened and I couldn't understand why it had run out. They were very happy by then from the *sake* and didn't seem to mind a bit, thinking it was actually quite funny.

Towards the end of the meal, one of the Italian ladies asked if I would mind taking a couple of photographs of the group. With four cameras in my hands, I backed out of their cubicle and collided with another waitress rushing back to the kitchen with a large black tray laden with dirty dishes — entirely my fault. There was an almighty crash, we both fell and dirty dishes and food remnants scattered everywhere. By this time, the Italians were howling with laughter. I was almost crying with embarrassment. I apologised profusely, helped gather up the dirty dishes, sent Emi on her way, gathered up the cameras, took their photos for them and fled. Thankfully, nothing further went wrong. As a gesture of amends when they were leaving, I deducted 10% from their bill and apologised once again. One of the men gave me a $20 tip and said with a huge boyish grin, 'Lady, that's the best night we've ever had!'

After that, my accidently blowing out a fluorescent light one night with a champagne cork seemed like nothing more than a minor irritation.

As I was cooking for two army girls seated by the lobster tank one night, Chef emerged from the kitchen with a tray to remove the lobster chosen from the tank by another patron. Just as he was returning to the kitchen, both of the girls covered their ears. Baffled, I asked them what they were doing. They replied that they had heard that lobsters scream when they are killed. That was a new one to me. I reassured them that they were killed humanely with a skewer to the brain and did not scream. That same night, there was a lot going on and all tables were occupied. One male diner decided he didn't want to pay for his dinner, and tried to sneak out via the fire escape at the rear of the restaurant. Hideki, a burly kitchen hand, happened to catch him and dragged him firmly by the collar, past shocked diners back through the restaurant to the Manager's Office in the front. The girls asked me what he had done. I replied straight-faced, 'That's what happens if you don't pay.' They both nodded vigorously and declared, 'We'll pay, we'll pay!'

We usually took delivery of a polystyrene box of live mud crabs before the dinner crowd trickled in, but occasionally the crabs would arrive late. On one such night, Chef decided to leave the crabs in the box until morning before placing them in the tank as it would not harm them to be left overnight. We came in at 10.00 the next morning to find eight mud crabs loose in the restaurant. Watching Chef and the kitchen hands trying to retrieve the unbound crabs without losing fingers was very entertaining for the rest of us and was the occasion of a lot of hilarity and teasing.

Occasionally, someone I knew would come in for a meal: a couple of old classmates from high school, my ex-Japanese teacher, Miss Atherton (with whom I am still in touch), and most embarrassingly, my dad.

Dad knew nothing about Japanese food, except that he thought it was nearly all raw. He asked that I choose for him, so I chose a couple of cooked dishes I thought would be more to his liking. When he began talking very loudly and saying that he demanded to see the Manager, and that his waitress was no good, I could have sunk through the floor with shame and embarrassment. Then he started laughing, but to me that was one joke that wasn't very funny. Considering we hadn't really been in touch since I'd left home and he'd left around the same time, I didn't know how I really felt about him being there. He could have jeopardised my job had the Manager been in one of his bad moods.

Singing at 'The Shoki'

Mr Tsukamoto had organised a *karaoke* (literally, 'empty orchestra') competition. It was an annual event, to be held on a Saturday night in the restaurant. The restaurant was closed to the public for the night; invited guests only. There were to be sections for male, female and duet (many popular Japanese songs were duets). One of the frequent diners at the restaurant, Mr Okada who worked for Datsun, had a really good voice and was keen to enter not only the male section but also the duet. He knew I had a good grasp of the language, and that I had sung at Tommy and Meredith's wedding and had something of a musical bent.

I agreed to enter the duet with Mr Okada with great trepidation. I had never sung in Japanese, and wasn't too keen on singing for a crowd of strangers. Mr Okada selected two songs: one for the two of us to sing as a duet, and another for me to do as a solo in the female section. He had already decided what he wanted to sing in the male section, and he had bucket-loads of confidence. I had only three weeks to learn both songs! Mr Okada came to the restaurant just on closing time each night for a week and a half, and patiently tutored me in both songs with the backing tapes and we would practise for about an hour or so each night. By closing time, I felt dead on my feet and it was a struggle to learn as much as I could in a very short time. There would be no referring to the lyrics — I had to know them both by heart. Some places with *karaoke* now have the lyrics appear on a screen for the singer to refer to, which removes a lot of stress, but not the *Shoki*. I was surprised that I learned most of the lyrics quite quickly. We were to sing '*Wakarete Mo Suki Na Hito*' (a love song about not forgetting a person the singer loved), '*Subaru*' (named for the Pleiades constellation — cars of the same make have the constellation as their logo/emblem), and I would sing '*Hoo Yoo*' (Embrace) by myself. The latter is a passionate love song with quite a difficult range. I learned it by heart, including inflection and breathing, and had to extend my usual vocal range upwards by about three extra notes. I needed help with some of the *kanji*, but otherwise was able to read the lyrics easily. Still, I pressed Mr Okada and one of the kitchen hands to translate most of the *kanji* as well so that I understood exactly what I was singing.

Mr Okada won the male section, we came second in the duet, and I came first in the female — there weren't very many female Japanese customers there that night. I was the only non-Japanese in the competition. One of the kitchen hands, Hideki, later said that he actually shed tears at my rendition of 'Hoo Yoo' because it reminded him of an old girlfriend. Several years later, in Japan, I won a *karaoke* competition in Osaka, that was scored by a machine (a '*tensu dasu kikai*' — score-giving-machine), and beat six Japanese with '*Hoo Yoo*'. They didn't need to know that I only knew just the two songs in Japanese! The Japanese man who came second was so disgruntled at being beaten by a foreigner, a woman, that I gave him my prize — a bottle of Chivas Regal — as a gesture of goodwill, which somewhat soothed his damaged pride. During the time I was working at the *Shoki*, I was living in a converted garage (minus shower and toilet, which were in the main house) in the backyard of a red brick house owned by a Polish man and his son, in Red Hill. At the restaurant we often finished work anywhere between midnight and 2 am, depending on how long it took our hints to induce lingering customers to leave. I used to walk home from the city, and never felt threatened or unsafe. Nothing could persuade me to do the same thing now as it would be inviting trouble.

I hadn't had any art lessons at that point, but had decided to use a sepia pastel pencil to create a jungle on one bare white wall of my garage palace. I would come home late, keyed up from work, and would add to my jungle a little at a time to wind down each night. As it happened, I moved out two weeks after I finished it and sometimes wonder if the next occupants kept it or painted over it.

A friend came to see me one Saturday morning with a newspaper clipping about a governess wanted in Japan, to teach two English missionaries' daughters aged eight and ten, and a couple of weekly English classes to Japanese children. I thought, why not apply? It was only for one year and in a backdoor kind of way, I would get to Japan to teach English as I'd always wanted to. Another major crossroad.

Working at the *Shoki* was one of my all-time favourite jobs, even though the pay wasn't great and I hated the split shifts. I was very sad to leave and I would really miss the *Shoki* 'family', but life in Japan beckoned.

A GAIJIN IN JAPAN

WEC

It has been said that you cannot cross a chasm in two jumps. Sometimes we are required to take a leap of faith. I applied for the position and was accepted to be governess for Dr McElligott and Mrs McElligott's two younger daughters, Ruth and Anne, in Ishiyama, which was about 40 minutes away by train from where I would be living.

The church I had been attending in Brisbane was very supportive of my going to Japan, even though I would only be there as a support worker, not as an actual missionary and the two roles were clearly delineated. They decided to partially fund me for the year I would be there, which was a surprise and solved my most pressing problem, as it was an unpaid position. The balance of my living expenses would come from English class fees

Six months before I was to leave for Japan, while living at Clayfield at WEC's Brisbane headquarters, I was afflicted by a mystery illness. I went to four doctors before one did a blood test and diagnosed me with Ross River Fever which I think I may have contracted in Townsville, where Sara and I had stayed in a mosquito-infested caravan park on our way back to Brisbane from the Gulf. At that time, only eight other cases had been diagnosed in Brisbane. Each previous doctor had told me it was only in my mind and that there was nothing wrong with me, before referring me to psychiatrists. The general aches and pains, and the knifing pains in my reflex joints of knees, wrists, ankles and elbows, general lethargy and fatigue were probably difficult to pin down as one particular disease. This looked like I may not be able to go to Japan after all. As it transpired, I returned a negative blood test just two days before I was due to leave for Osaka. A great leap across the chasm.

I don't think my parents were thrilled by my going to Japan, but they were both at Brisbane airport to see me off. They hadn't been overly happy about me going to live in the Outback either, but having both lived in country areas for some time themselves, accepted it. At least in the Outback, I had been in the same country. I cried for the greater part of the flight to Osaka, thinking, 'Oh my God, what have I done?' The poor steward fussed over me, frequently asking if he could bring me anything or do anything for me, having already brought me two glasses of water and a blanket. Visiting Japan was one thing, but living there for a whole year away from friends and family with even more restricted contact was going to be something of a challenge. My father mumbled, 'I bet you'll come home married to some slitty-eyed little bugger.' He made it perfectly clear that not only was he not keen on my living in Japan but he definitely did not want a Japanese son-in-law.

When I arrived in Osaka, I was met by Richard Owens, one of the senior missionaries with WEC in Shiga prefecture.

WEC stood for Worldwide Evangelisation for Christ. I was to live in the organisation's headquarters in rural Gokasho for the first seven months, undertake general duties at the mission headquarters, teach English in another small village called Yookaiichi six kilometres away on Saturdays, and travel by train five days a week to the McElligotts' home in Ishikawa, some forty minutes or so away. After the first seven months, I would be living in Kusatsu with Jenny Fletcher in a small flat and would commute to the McElligotts from there. It was October — autumn, the leaves were just beginning to turn and the nights and mornings were distinctly chilly. The concept of four individual seasons was a wonderful novelty to someone who had only lived in the sub-tropics and the harsh Outback Australian climate.

Around 2 o'clock in the morning of my second day at the *hombu* (headquarters), I experienced my first earthquake. It felt as though someone was shaking me by the shoulder. Couldn't fall out of bed — I was sleeping on the floor. I called out to Rhonda (who had been in Japan some twenty years), 'Rhonda, Rhonda, is that an earthquake?' Her drowsy reply was, 'Yes, go back to sleep!' That was the first of 33 earth tremors and quakes I experienced in the five years I was in the country, the largest of which was a 6.3 on the Richter Scale. That was strong enough to shake high-rises in the cities and cause significant damage from falling debris. Although it is possible to get used to them, they were still scary, especially if one was in a high-rise building. If travelling in public transport or a car, one can barely feel the lower scale tremors. They were discussed much as the weather was.

'Wasn't that a bad fog this morning?'

'Did you feel the tremors last night where you were?'

Rhonda Sallaway was the only missionary who lived permanently in the old farm house that was WEC's headquarters. It was huge, old and rambling. I counted 17 rooms, many of which could be opened together to make larger rooms and a variety of configurations. There was a walled Japanese-style garden that had gone to seed — such a shame, one old Japanese-style pit toilet which was emptied monthly by the ever-cheerful *kumotori* man and his truck with its suction pipe. And, joy of joys — a *wooden* Japanese bath made from fragrant cedar. In winter, especially, it was a heavenly indulgent treat to spend half an hour or so soaking up to my neck in blissfully hot water, when it was snowing or blowing a gale outside. The wooden floors of the corridors gleamed with a dull sheen. Water from the bath, full of skin oils of the bathers, had been used since the house was built a hundred or so years before to clean the wooden floors and impart to them their lovely glow.

For my weekends, after I moved to Kusatsu, I was to live with Rhonda and help with general and administrative duties, as well as teaching my Saturday classes in nearby Yookaiichi. Linda had a superb command of the Japanese language and nuance and on the telephone, most people could not pick her from a Japanese. She was a valuable mentor during my first year living in Japan.

In the garden were a prolific fig tree and a fan-leafed *gingko* tree among other plants. It was delightful to watch the foliage change through the seasons, and in summer, to pluck fresh, ripe figs from the tree for dessert. In winter, the icicles that clung to the eaves measured about half a metre, and the snow in the garden was hip deep. When the missionaries' kids came to visit, they used to love to break off the icicles and have mock sword fights with them, clowning around in the snow drifts. I moved from sleeping in one of the eight mat upstairs rooms from which I had a magnificent view of a snow-capped mountain and rice fields, to the *kura*, which, when the house was built, would have been the granary. The walls were half a metre thick, with no windows. I was working on the theory that with thicker walls, it should be warmer than the room I had been using. The howling winter wind had no flimsy wood and paper panels there to force its way between. I had an electric blanket which in Japan are made to lie over the sleeper, not under as in Australia. Yet I would still wake with a line of tiny icicles on the edge of my *kakebuton* where my breath had touched it, condensed and frozen during the night.

After seven months of commuting long distances, I moved to Kusatsu to share a flat with Jenny, who was teaching the nearby Dutch/Australian Van der Hyde children. I only travelled to the *hombu* on weekends after that. I had a tiny room of just three mats in the flat I shared. The Japanese measure room size by mats, which are a standard size of about 1.5m by 90cm. The only furniture in it were a small chest of drawers and a kerosene heater. In the close confines I often bumped the heater, so it was a good thing that Japanese kerosene heaters are made with a cut-out switch that automatically turns them off in case of earthquakes or accidentally falling over. Jenny's room was opposite mine on the first floor, which, just to confuse things, is the second floor in Japan and the Ground Floor is the First Floor; USA influence. The ground floor consisted of a Japanese-style flush toilet, a small bathroom with a cube-shaped Japanese bath, and our kitchen/laundry/dining room/classroom which had a table and four chairs. It was adequate for us and we lived there happily enough.

One afternoon, soon after I had moved to Kusatsu, Kees Van der Hyde brought me a rather beaten-up white bicycle.

To my blank look he replied, 'Well, you can ride, can't you?'

'No. I've never ridden a bicycle'.

Dutch people are practically born on bicycles, and I think Kees was a bit confused by the fact that I couldn't ride — even his two-year-old toddler could. Jenny undertook to teach me, on the street outside our flat.

Next door to the flats was a miniscule gravelled park surrounded by wire fencing, where seniors played Gateball — similar to croquet. I hit the fence. I hit a telegraph pole. I fell off. I finally went straight! To my utter embarrassment, the ten or so old people in the park halted their game and stood by the fence, hanging their fingers in the wire gaps, egging me on with shouts of *'gambatte ne!'* (stick at it, go for it!) and loud clapping. I'll bet it made for some amusing dinner conversation that evening.

So, in theory, I had mastered a new skill. There was an old-style heavy-duty bicycle at the headquarters, which even until now, is the most comfortable bike I have ever ridden. It was painted dark green, had solid rubber tyres, old-style handles and brakes, and a frame so heavy that I could barely lift it. I also had the seat down as low as it could go. The cracked leather seat was generous in size, suited to my large gaijin bum. I had to travel to my English classes by bus, until later when I had learned to ride. Then I was able to ride the *hombu* bike to and from my classes at Yookaiichi with confidence. There were two routes to the church hall where I taught. I used to like to ride through the forest that hugged the rice fields as it was so dim and peaceful, quiet and cool in summer, and the other was a purpose-built bike pathway alongside the main road.

Sometimes I met farmers or other people on the way who used the bike path to access their fields. One time I rode along behind an old man walking along with two buckets of sewage slung from a wooden yoke over his narrow shoulders (the stench was terrible and was more than likely human excrement), destined for his vegetables — there was simply no room to pass him. Another time, I met an old lady who had spread her sesame seeds out on woven straw mats in the middle of the path to dry. I dismounted, greeted her, and as I was in no hurry that morning, was given an impromptu lecture from her on the process of growing and preparing sesame seeds. The little shrines along the forest path were mostly dedicated to Jizo, the god who looked after the 'water children' — babies who died in the womb, were aborted, stillborn or who died shortly after birth. At different times of the year the statues of Jizo were draped in red fabric aprons. The sad thing was that these statues and tiny shrines showed signs of being tended frequently. I was usually late coming back to the *hombu* because I would stop and look at things or converse with people I met along the way.

Going to another country only to teach would be arrogant. Living in a foreign country is a constant learning experience, both good and bad. I learned as much, if not more, from my students than they ever learned from me. The local church ran English classes for children, and for housewives. The kids' classes were a lot of fun, although attendance rates plummeted dramatically in baseball season as the children attended mandatory after-school sports practice.

The children ranged in age from five to eleven, and were shy, but eager to learn. The emphasis was on spoken English. Japanese children learn English at school, but mostly sound like they are speaking in *katakana* (Japanese alphabet for foreign and onomatopoeic words). For example, 'I'm fine, thank you,' becomes *'Ai amu fuain, san kyu'*. The majority of Japanese English teachers speak very poor English, and so learning from a native speaker is very desirable. Of the foreigners who go to Japan to work, 99% of them work as English teachers in one form or another, the rest work on the ski fields, for multinational corporations, or in sleazy but well-paying 'hostess bars'. One time I did a double take when a Japanese man spoke to me in English with a thick Scottish accent — his English teacher had been a Scotsman. I wonder how many Japanese I have left with an Australian accent?

'My' kids were very solicitous of my wellbeing, demonstrated especially one day when going to class I misjudged a curve in the road and cycled right off the edge into a snow drift up to my chest. I was wet and shivering by the time I made it to class. The kids pulled up a stool to the kerosene heater for me, and two kids ran all the way home to fetch an assortment of dry clothes for me to borrow. There was a lot of giggling at my expense, but I thought it funny, too. The incident did wonders for my relationship with the kids.

Teaching the primary school aged McElligott children was delightful. They were happy, well-adjusted girls, who, even though their first language was English, would use Japanese unconsciously as their 'play language', having spent most of their short lives in Japan. They were very Japanese in their habits and mannerisms. I learned a lot about aspects of Japanese culture and language from them that I never could have from books.

To my surprise, for a country that boasts almost zero graffiti, some people get their kicks in other ways. Sometimes I would leave the train and find my bicycle amongst the hundreds of others parked near the station, only to find that the top of the bell had been stolen, or even worse, the entire seat — rendering the bicycle useless. It was difficult to steal an actual bicycle because Japanese bicycles are fitted with front wheel keyed locks that when locked prevented the front wheel from moving at all. If they had these locks in Australia, I have no doubt that someone bent on stealing a bike would figure out a way to disable the lock.

My old white bicycle had come from what we jokingly called the 'Roadside Shopping Centre' or *oogata gomi* — big garbage — that people put on the side of the road when they upgrade to a new model, or they simply don't want any more.

There is almost no such thing in Japan as storage space or secondhand shops. Later, when I moved to Osaka, I furnished my entire flat from the Roadside Shopping Centre — washing machine, fridge, chest of drawers, table, some pots and pans, two Japanese-style legless chairs, a *kotatsu* (low table with quilt around it and heater underneath), a stereo, and light fittings — all in perfect working order.

On my day off, I used to ride up into the hills around a small town called Ritto, and not worry if I became lost because I could always ask directions in Japanese. I would pack lunch, sketchpad and camera and off I would go. Deliberately losing myself and going where whim and fancy took me like this, I met some very interesting people whose paths I would not normally have crossed. One chilly day, I was sitting on the edge of a rice field sketching it and the mountains dusted with snow beyond, when an old lady with a limp and an ancient bicycle stopped and asked me in gruff Japanese what I was doing there.

'I'm sorry, is this your rice field? I was just sketching it because it is very pretty with the mountains behind it.'

'Yes it is. I think you had better come home with me and have some tea. My son speaks English. He works for a bank. He'll be home soon for lunch.'

I met the son, whose English was limited to 'Harro'. After we had green tea and made conversation, which consisted mostly of me answering their curious questions about Australia and what I was doing in Japan, in Japanese. The old lady, Mrs Nakamura, gave me a shopping bag full of homemade pickled radish, which I really like — in very small quantities. I had to endure the ripe, pungent aroma from the basket on the front of my bicycle all the way home, but I made my neighbours very happy when I shared it.

Sometimes, Japanese would comment on my good grasp of the language and accent and would ask if one of my parents was Japanese or if I was born in Japan. I am about as Caucasian as it is possible to be: fair skin, dark hair and blue eyes. With a straight face and if I was in a wicked mood, I would respond that I was from one of the blue-eyed Ainu tribes from Hokkaido, northern Japan. They would nod and accept this explanation with a slow, '*ah, naruhodo desu ne*' (ah, of course). Most of the Japanese in the south have little idea about or interest in the northern native Ainu people who once thrived in Hokkaido, the northern-most of the four main Japanese islands.

On another occasion, it was a cold autumn day and I purchased a can of hot coffee from a vending machine outside a tiny shop, in a crooked laneway of an ancient hillside village. I was warming my hands with the hot can when the sliding door opened and a very old Japanese lady, bent almost double under the weight of her considerable age, invited me in to warm myself by the *hibachi*. She was delighted to find that I spoke the language and asked many questions about where I was from and what I was doing. I was also able to ask about her life and family. When I told her I was from Australia, she looked very solemn, bowed so low that her forehead touched the *tatami* mat, and began apologising to me for World War II. I told her gently that my parents were born at the end of the war, that it was two generations ago and mostly there were no hard feelings except from older people in Australia who had experienced the war firsthand. It should be remembered that for the average Japanese, the war was a very difficult time too, with hunger, shortages, loss of loved ones, and other problems. Some Japanese, however, were militant and were very susceptible to the ideologies spouted by the Japanese propaganda machine.

A Kid Called 'Shut Up'

New missionaries were always coming and going at the *hombu* and some of the more memorable ones were a black guy from Zimbabwe, Newman Mzvondiwa, and a German couple named Heinz and Ilsa. The latter had a two-year old girl named Damaris. The Japanese reacted first in shock and then with laughter. 'Damaris' is very close to the Japanese words for 'Shut the hell up!' Damaris was a cute little girl but seemed to be everywhere all at once. She was intrigued by the twenty or so pairs of indoor slippers at the entry to the *hombu*. One by one, she picked them up, and unnoticed carried them down the corridor and dropped them down the pit toilet, as she was obviously fascinated by the sound they made as they splashed on the bottom. Her parents were absolutely mortified, and had to pay for another twenty pairs of indoor slippers. Shoes were left at the door; indoor slippers were used indoors and up to the toilet door; the indoor slippers were usual fluffy or fabric, and were exchanged for vinyl toilet slippers which are worn only in the toilet. The process is reversed when exiting the toilet. Slippers are never worn in tatami matted rooms, only socks, stockings or bare feet are acceptable there.

My one memory of Newman was of him sitting on a large rock in the garden, playing his guitar ... with the toilet slippers on! We didn't know whether to tell him of his mistake or not, but felt duty-bound to educate him in Japanese etiquette. Eventually someone did tell him and it never happened again. Such are the pitfalls of life in the big Nippon. People frequently don't tell you of the mistakes you make as a foreigner which means that there is the potential to continue making the same ones over and over for the entire length of your stay there.

Richard and Edna Owens had been missionaries in Japan for years, and in fact the youngest of their five children had been born in Japan. Richard was English and Edna was American. Edna's obstetrician had been Japanese. When Japanese babies are born, they usually have a full head of hair. When Edna's baby's head crowned, the doctor flew into a panic and tried to figure out why the tests hadn't shown it would be a breach birth. Maia was born as bald as a bowling ball. The doctor ended up quite confused and embarrassed, having mistaken Maia's head for her behind.

Once a month there would be a day-long meeting of the missionaries at the *hombu* for fellowship, business and a meal. Cooking for thirty or forty people in a tiny Japanese kitchen with a mere two gas burners, and limited refrigeration, was a challenge. When we all met together though, the food was generally a very simple rice dish and a piece of fruit. These monthly meetings were partly for us to spend time speaking in English that did not come from a textbook, even though English was not necessarily the native language of all of us.

We had German, Zimbabwean, Dutch, Australian, American and French missionaries, but English was the *lingua franca*.

God Loves Carrots

The Van der Hyde children that Jenny taught spent a lot of time with the neighbourhood kids and spoke Japanese as their play language. Add that to Dutch, and English, and you have some very smart linguistically adaptable kids. However, little children have no difficulty differentiating among the different languages they speak and are able to switch from one to another as the situation demands. I tried to learn a little Dutch from Kees, but failed dismally, because I couldn't manage the deep guttural tones.

Kees had Jenny and me in stitches one afternoon as he told us of some of the well-known mistakes made by missionaries in their preaching in Japan. One minister preached that God loves carrots, when he used the word *ninjin* (carrots) instead of *ningen* (people). Another entreated his parishioners to leave behind their filthy wives (*tsuma*) instead of sin (*tsumi*), and turn to God with rats (*nezumi*) instead of hope (*nozomi*) in their hearts. The interpreter for another minister interpreted the entire sermon as being that King David's secret was that he was angry with God, instead of 'hungry for God'. The minister would have been none the wiser, except that the interpreter asked him later at lunch what he had meant about

David being angry at God. The minister had wondered about the strange looks on the congregation's faces. These were good warnings to be careful in what we said.

The Traffic Accident

My Japanese friends taught me to save money by shopping seasonally at local markets, and by doing so, I could eat quite well. Food in season there was delicious, fresh and cheap. One day I took some photographs of the wonderful variety of seafood in the seafood market, for friends at home. A man came out from his stall waving his arms and yelling, 'No *furashi*, no *furashi*'. Apparently, the flash photography might disturb the dead fish, octopi and other seafood. Or maybe he thought I was a secret agent working for a rival fishmonger. I still don't know.

One morning I was cycling to the railway station down the market street, part of my usual morning commute. A six-year-old boy on a bicycle was pedalling furiously towards me on the wrong side, did a right-angled turn in front of me (he later said that he was shocked by the fact that I was a *gaijin* and panicked). All I could see were two huge round eyes, a baseball cap tilted back and two front teeth like uncut blocks of *tofu*. The bikes collided and we were both thrown onto the road. There was a policeman standing nearby, probably bored out of his mind, and he decided that since there were two 'vehicles' involved, it constituted a traffic accident. I thought I had broken my hip as it hurt like hell. The little boy sustained a small cut above one eye, which needed two small stitches.

By coincidence, my landlady was in the nearby post office and when she heard that a *gaijin* had been hurt nearby, she thought to go outside and see if it was one of 'her' *gaijin*. She was wonderful and took charge of everything. I was in shock and my Japanese language deserted me completely. I was taken to a nearby hospital for X-rays while the little boy was attended to. The boy's father came and very magnanimously said that he would not make me pay for the boy's medical treatment. I was incensed at his attitude since it was his child that had caused the accident. I learned an immutable Japanese law that day — if a child and adult are involved in an accident, it is automatically the adult's fault, never the child's. The police wanted me to come to the police station the following day. I could barely walk (no broken bones, only a lot of very colourful and painful bruising) but went to the police station all the same. I was asked to make a statement and was fingerprinted. I had to show my Alien Registration Card which all non-Japanese must carry at all times. The police decided to treat it as a genuine accident, and no further action was taken. I think that up until that moment, the novelty and nuisance value of a gaijin being involved broke the monotony of their day-to-day work. I was admonished not to cause any more accidents. So, when asked if I have a police record now, I have to reply yes, and no.

We Are Going to Cause You Trouble

Something that causes people anywhere a lot of angst is when a building project begins next door. In Australia, we grin and bear it, or complain to the owner/builder/council if it drives us nuts. The unmelodious sound of jackhammers or pile drivers at 7 in the morning is not an ideal start to one's day. Most people would prefer the lesser annoyance of their alarm clocks any day.

In Japan, they have hit upon an ingenious solution to a worldwide problem: you tell the neighbours *before* you start building. By warning the neighbours in advance that you are going to cause them trouble with noise, dirt, concrete dust, workmen swarming all over the site, trucks coming and going, etc., you obviate the right to complain. Cut off the annoyed person at the knees, if you will. The foreman or owner buys boxes of cakes and visits each of the neighbours in turn. He apologises for the mess and the noise, asks that you forgive them in advance and hands you a box of cakes.

When Jenny and I found out that a new block of flats was to be built behind our block in Kusatsu, and that it would be right on the edge of the rice field behind us, we were not happy, but felt powerless to do anything, especially since the owner did exactly what Japanese builders do, and dutifully brought us a box of cakes. Jenny and I complained to Kees and Lydia Van der Hyde about the nuisance it was going to cause and he asked us if we had received any cakes. We were surprised and replied that yes, as a matter of fact we had.

'Case closed,' said Kees. 'By accepting them, you have undertaken not to complain or cause the builder and owner any grief.'

Another Lesson in Japanese Efficiency

The Japanese are incredibly innovative when it comes to getting around problems or potential problems. Another example is that Japanese will tell you that there is no pornography in Japan. I soon found that such a blanket statement was not only incorrect but also blatantly obvious when pornographic magazines could be purchased from vending machines at railway stations and outside shops. This meant that it was even available to children — anyone, in fact, who had change in their pocket. I asked some Japanese friends about this and was told matter-of-factly that as long as there was no pubic hair showing, it was not considered to be pornographic. From what I saw, the magazines were certainly pornographic by Australian standards. Once again, a simple razor removes a potential problem. No pubic hair, no problem. The *definition* is the key, and this applies in business dealings with Japanese as well.

In older times in Japan, when the tenets of Buddhism were adhered to perhaps more strictly, most Japanese did not eat red meat. However, as the whale was considered to be a fish rather than a mammal, whale meat was commonly sold at market. (Japanese whaling in the Southern Ocean now angers me, because I have seen whale meat for sale in markets. So much for their insistence that they only kill them for scientific purposes.) Hungry Japanese in days past would catch wild boar for the table, nicknaming it 'mountain whale' if anybody asked, thus breaching no Buddhist or Shintoist tenets.

Nude Neighbours

I had met Malcolm Masters in Australia at a seminar. He worked in Japan for an organisation called 'World Outreach', an interdenominational Christian organisation involved in setting up churches in and around Osaka, educating and training pastors, and humanitarian works. They also offered English classes for various age and interest groups. He would be in Osaka for a couple of years as the Japan Director of World Outreach.

Just as my year with WEC was ending and I was preparing to return to Australia, I had a phone call from Malcolm in Osaka, asking if I would consider staying on, but moving to Osaka to become his Personal Assistant. I had never done any serious office work before, and so replied, 'Don't be silly, I can't even type!' His three-word response set me on a new course: 'You can learn.' How often does an expression of faith in one's ability alter the direction of their life? If only we had the faith in ourselves that others have in us, we could probably accomplish so much more.

I borrowed a twenty-five-year-old manual typewriter and with an instruction book I bought from an English language bookshop in Kyoto, I taught myself to touch-type by practising every night for two months. It was extremely rare for a mission worker in Japan to be granted a change of visa from one organisation to another. Everyone expected that it would be denied and that we would have a fight on our hands, but the transfer was made quickly and without incident, thank God.

One major difference between WEC and World Outreach was that the WEC missionaries felt that Japanese language lessons would be wasted on anyone who was not a frontline missionary, thus limiting the effectiveness of people like me in dealing with Japanese people on a day-to-day basis. I thought this was very short-sighted, and Rhonda helped me organise a private one-on-one class twice a week with Mrs Nagata, who lived nearby and whom I paid directly instead of through WEC. In contrast, World Outreach, felt that all mission workers should be learning the language for as long as they were in the country. Consequently, when I moved to Osaka, transferring from WEC to World Outreach, I commenced classes at the YMCA Japanese Language School in central Osaka, and was really happy with the level and content of the classes. It also meant that I was able to readily converse in Japanese with my classmates from Sudan, Korea, Iran, France, Germany and Switzerland, as we all had very good Japanese skills.

The first place I lived in Osaka was at Pension Yamaguchi in Toyonaka. It was dormitory-style accommodation for singles. My room was a reasonable eight mats in size and had a kitchenette with two gas burners and a fridge that had seen better days. At that time, ovens were very rare, mostly because Japanese home cooking doesn't require one.

Japanese kitchens were tiny and there was simply no room for the space required by an oven. There were little toaster ovens available, but I never had the knack of using one to cook things like cakes. The toilets were down the hallway, and the bathhouse was down the street and around a corner. This was not an unusual arrangement.

The first few times I went to the bathhouse, I was embarrassed, and the other women, ALL Japanese, stared openly. Apparently, I was the first foreigner to visit that particular bathhouse, according to the conversations I listened to. The Japanese ladies were amazed by the fact that my white skin would turn vivid pink and red after being immersed in the water which was just a fraction below boiling point. For my first few visits, I feigned ignorance of the language so that I could listen to the ladies' candid comments. One time though, I laughed at a joke one of the ladies made, meaning that I had accidentally let it be known that I could speak the language. Suddenly, I was part of the neighbourhood. We would chat while washing. One old lady used to want to wash my back and then it was expected that I would return the favour. She was a tiny and an obviously respected elder of my neighbourhood. I took this as a gracious sign of acceptance. There's nothing like stripping all your clothes off to get acquainted with the neighbours. Sometimes the local ladies would greet me in the street and I wouldn't recognise them immediately with their clothes on and hair neatly coiffed.

On one occasion, I had a friend named Vanessa visiting me from Brisbane. When I told her she would have to go to the public bathhouse with me, she freaked out completely. Vanessa said that she would rather stay dirty. It was the height of summer and she was sharing my room. My way or the highway. The *O-furoba* (bathhouse) has the same rules as bathing at home in Japan: wash first at the bank of taps while sitting on small plastic stools about 20 centimetres high, rinse off and only then was it okay to soak in the bath. Bathhouses are a social institution, as well as being for cleansing. People tend to relax and take their time. Anything under an hour raises eyebrows.

At my local bathhouse, there were three separate baths (each large enough for about eight people at one time) a very hot bath, a cold bath, and another unique to the area — an electricity bath. There was low voltage electricity pulsing through the water, and there was a sign on the wall in Japanese above it warning that if you had a weak heart, you should not use that bath. Think back to the time as a child when you stuck your tongue on the top of a nine-volt radio battery, just to see what it was like. Well, the sensation in the *biribiri* bath was like that. Before I had time to warn her, Vanessa stepped into that bath, screamed and jumped out again. Much to her acute embarrassment, every eye in the place turned in her direction. She didn't forgive me. At the front entry of the bathhouse sat an elderly man to take the fees as bathers came in from the street. He was usually reading porn magazines. If he wanted to see real live nudes, all he had to do was turn around. I thought it was hilarious, unless, of course, he was reading it for the articles (yeah, right). Vanessa did not return to the bathhouse, and given her acute embarrassment, I couldn't blame her, and left her to her ablutions at the kitchen sink for the rest of the visit. She *had* said that she wanted to see what real life in Japan was like.

My favourite time of year was winter. It was wonderful to cycle through the snowy streets as evening fell, soak in the near-boiling water at the bath house, dress quickly and then cycle home again with steam billowing from my clothes into the frigid air. I would dive into my futon as soon as I had kicked my shoes off, and be toasty warm for the rest of the night. I had a little kerosene heater but it didn't really do much to warm the one room flat at Pension Yamaguchi. It was also common to see people riding their bicycles through the snow-silenced streets, with an open umbrella grasped in one hand to save being covered by snow. I was quite proud of myself when I mastered this trick.

Native speakers of English are a valuable commodity in Japan, and some *gaijin* find that the language unlocks many doors that would not normally be open to them in their mother countries. Mrs Yamaguchi had a friend who owned a sizable Japanese-style restaurant. He wanted the menu translated into English in an effort to attract foreign customers. There weren't too many foreigners in the area, but I respected his efforts all the same. Mrs Yamaguchi had organised for the two of us to visit the restaurant one evening, so that I could begin work on the menu she had agreed I would translate. We sat at a table for three with the owner. I began by asking for descriptions of each dish, so that I could then describe them in English. When I came to a dish on the menu with which I was unfamiliar, he would clap his hands in the direction of the kitchen, the head chef would come running out with a brisk, 'hai' and a few minutes later the dish would appear on the table, as if Tanaka-san had conjured a genie whose sole purpose was to grant our culinary wishes. I appreciated this fact very quickly, and cunningly asked for a couple of my favourite dishes as well, not betraying the fact that I knew exactly what these dishes were! I dutifully finished the menu, and then typed up the new menu in both English and Japanese. As I had a Japanese word-processor, and was pretty good at *kanji*, the task was not too onerous. It was a unique experience and one that I enjoyed immensely.

There was a Japanese girl who was an air hostess with JAL living in the Pension, too. She was away quite a lot. However, when she was home, she and I would sit on the back steps of the Pension and play together — Reiko on her flute and me on my mandolin. It sounded pretty good and a lot of the other residents would emerge from their rooms to listen. Mostly, I can hear a piece once or twice and then play it. The mandolin is a great instrument for either melody or harmony. My guitar and mandolin playing, and singing, were mostly limited to church on a Sunday, so this was just for fun.

Malcolm was not only tall and had the scars on his forehead to prove it, (from repeatedly crashing into low beams) but he also had flaming red hair and a red beard. One particular day, he wanted a haircut and beard trim. I made an appointment for him with my hairdresser and accompanied him in case there were any communication difficulties. My hairdressers were a young married couple. When my boss came in, the wife nearly fainted. She managed to cut his hair, but when it came to the beard, she just kept saying 'No, no, no,' and had to ask her husband to do it as she had never trimmed a beard in her life, let alone a thick, curly red one, which looked to have the texture of barbed wire. The whole incident was very funny from my point of view. Perhaps my hairdressers were afraid that they were gaining an unwanted reputation as *gaijin* hairdressers. They became such good friends that I sometimes had them around to my room for dinner. Japanese rarely invite people to their homes for dinner, but usually go to a *kissaten* or restaurant to catch up with friends as many Japanese are not only embarrassed about the small size of their living quarters, but feel on a more equal social footing if they invite their guests to dine out with them in neutral territory.

I loved living at Pension Yamaguchi near the Toyonaka railway station. Mrs Yamaguchi was delightful. Her husband worked nights in a bakery, and that meant that she had to stay up until 11.30 pm each night when the outer doors had to be locked. I had to pass her apartment at the bottom of the single flight of wooden stairs. She would be listening for me and would beckon me into her front room as I was coming in after a long day. She would often prepare a meal or snack for me, and we would talk in Japanese on a wide range of subjects, often until the early hours of the morning. She was very lonely with her husband away at night and her ten-year-old son asleep. I learned more from her than from any of the language classes I took at the YMCA Language School in central Osaka or other source.

Something that Mrs Yamaguchi told me still sticks in my mind as being particularly funny; something I could never have learned from a book. Japanese women do not look forward to their husbands retiring. A retired husband with nothing to do is called by women '*gokiburi teishu*' which means 'cockroach husbands' — always under foot and where they are least wanted. Japan has also been likened to an onion: it is like layers and layers and the more one peels off, the more is revealed underneath. No one mentions the fact that Japan can also make you cry.

Parcels from home were wonderful. Mrs Yamaguchi derived a vicarious pleasure from watching me open them and would be really excited on my behalf whenever one arrived for me from Australia. My mother used to send me one of her boiled fruitcakes twice a year — for Christmas and my birthday in June. She sent it by airmail the first time. It was almost 6 kg and the cost of postage was at least $40 dollars. One morning, I took Mum's newly-arrived, foil-wrapped cake to my ladies' English/cooking class, passed it around and asked the ladies to guess what it was. Most guesses were that it was some kind of stone, as Mum's fruitcakes were very dense and heavy. I then unwrapped it and gave them all a slice. They liked it and it was radically different than Japanese fruit cake, which consists of a Madeira cake with half a handful of sultanas in the bottom. Mum's fruitcake was one of the things I missed most about Australia, along with grass beneath my feet and the sound of butcher birds, and magpies in the morning. I would share it (small pieces only) with my New Zealand and Australian work colleagues, then eke it out crumb by crumb to make it last. After the first cake, subsequent ones took the three-month journey by sea, for a much cheaper postage fee. It occurred to me at the time that there were at least three items that would not sell in Japan: lawnmowers, bubble bath and shoelaces.

Other things I needed to have sent from home were underwear and shoes. My feet are half a centimetre bigger than the longest Japanese ladies' shoes. I tried to buy a bra from a lingerie shop and was laughed out of the store. The flat-chested store dummy in the window should have been a dead giveaway. The two attendants just burst into peals of laughter (which, to be fair, in Japan can simply mean they are embarrassed). So I left empty-handed. A friend sent me a clipping from a Brisbane newspaper about the difficulties faced by bustier Australian models trying without success to crack the lucrative Japanese market. The witty tongue-in-cheek headline read *Good Golly Big Dolly, So Sorry*.

On my birthday one year, I was shopping at a local food store when I came upon a lonely, shrivelled passionfruit. I had never before seen one for sale in any of the stores or stalls in the local Japanese market. Since it *was* my birthday, I decided I would buy myself the passionfruit as a birthday present. The girl on the checkout asked me what it was as she had not seen one before. She had to find the manager in order to ask the price. Perhaps it was the fact that I was a foreigner, but the price was a shocking eight Australian dollars! I ate that passionfruit seed by seed and relished each tiny burst of flavour. Friends at home received this story with great incredulity. Later, when I returned to Australia on furlough, a friend who had passionfruit growing in wild profusion on her back fence brought me a plastic shopping bag full of the fruit. I gorged myself on them until it came to the point where my body said 'Enough!' and I didn't care if I never saw another one.

Some vegetables that were unknown in Japan at that time, were zucchinis and red capsicums. I didn't particularly miss either of them, but it was strange to me that the vegetables to which I was accustomed, were absent from the markets. Unusual to me, however, were the okra, and small eggplant. I couldn't find recipes for either, so once again turned to my Japanese housewife friends.

Some summer afternoons on days off, I would sit outside the Pension on the steps in the shade of a large tree chatting with one or two other residents, fanning ourselves in the suffocating high humidity. I seemed to be a magnet for all of the kids of the neighbourhood. Word quickly spread that I spoke Japanese. Up to ten kids at a time would congregate around me, asking me about Australia, what it was like, what the animals were like, and sometimes quite personal questions. They also loved to share their games, particularly the one that involves shaking the hand out to form rock, paper or scissors. Just to confuse the issue and see how they reacted, I added one of my own: string (the index finger held horizontally). String can wrap stone or paper, but scissors can cut string, I explained. This confused the kids until they realised I was joking with them, and they all thought it was a great addition to the traditional three options. Another *gaijin* told me he added 'dynamite' — the index finger pointing straight up and that dynamite beats everything else and made the kids in his classes laugh till they cried. Another of the kids' favourite games was '*yubizumo*' or finger wrestling. To play, you clasp hands with your opponent, leaving the thumbs free. Each person tries to push down the other's thumb. The one on top wins. As with the previous game, this one can also be used to quickly settle disputes. Everyone knows that the rules brook no argument, so every player is on the same page from the beginning.

Sitting like this on a particularly steamy afternoon, one of the kids said, 'Jessie-san, why do you have such a high nose?' In Japan, a large or prominent nose is referred to as being high. I replied that I had pre-ordered it from God before I was born so that I would have somewhere to perch my glasses. The kids nodded as though this explanation made perfect sense. On other occasions, the kids would bring their pet cicadas and crickets in tiny bamboo cages, for me to admire. I really enjoyed my time with the little kids — they are so honest and transparent, and say exactly what they think without censoring it through the filters of what was socially accepted. A little boy with his mother was waiting for his grandmother. When she arrived, he excitedly told her, 'Grandma, Grandma, I've been talking to the foreign lady in English!' I guess his logic dictated that he must have been speaking English since we had had a conversation and he had understood what I was saying. Many of these children ended up in my English classes and were quite relaxed because they already knew me.

Pension Yamaguchi was just one street from the railway station, and the floor, glass cupboard doors and windows would all shake when a train went past. The only respite was between midnight and 5 am. It took a while to become used to it, and sometimes I couldn't sleep until I had counted the trains and heard the last passenger or freight train rattle noisily by. Added to the noise and rumblings from the trains, the Japanese guy in the room below mine was trying to teach himself to play classical guitar at night. He only ever played one particular classical piece but would make a mistake and then go back to the beginning and start again, and again. It was really annoying and used to set my teeth on edge. Mrs Yamaguchi used to call him '*petagon*' behind his back (*peta* from '*petapeta*' — the slap slap of indoor slippers on wood — and *gon* from a word for a large lizard or dinosaur). I have no idea what the classical piece was called, but if I hear it anywhere now, I have to clench my teeth or leave the room. The first time I realised the severity of the effect it had on me was when it began to play just after I had placed an order in a café. The wait staff must have thought I was mad when I stood abruptly with a pained expression on my face and fled!

One of my favourite English classes near Toyonaka comprised five children aged five and six, and a rabbit. The class was held at the home of two of the children, and they would bring their pet rabbit to class. The rabbit was housetrained, and showed an inquisitive interest in what the kids were doing. I worked the kids hard, and they were sharp, with very retentive minds. I kept the pace fast with lots of games and achieved what I thought were amazing results with them. I would ask them to tell me answers to specific questions about the rabbit in English, which they had no trouble doing. The Englishman who took over the class from me said they were the best group of kids in terms of English conversational ability that he had encountered in Japan.

While I was living in Toyonaka, the handle on my mandolin case broke. I had heard there was a second-hand shop, which were very rare then, out near the Osaka airport. It took me a while to find it and I was the only customer there in the disarray and serendipitously grouped objects against the dusty glass windows and walls. In one corner of the shop, behind a small table, I spotted an old Neapolitan mandolin case and had to investigate. The price was 1,000 yen (about ten dollars then), which I thought was a bit steep for a battered mandolin case which had a broken lock. However, the handle would be a good match for my case. I picked up the case and it fell open, revealing a very old Neapolitan-style mandolin.

Upon examination it proved to be a 1910 Raffaele Calace mandolin, numbered on the inside. It was missing some strings and needed some work, but I couldn't pay fast enough, knowing that this was an incredible find. The shop owner gave me 500 yen back and said, 'Here, dear, get yourself a cup of coffee.' I excitedly took it home, cleaned off years of accumulated grime, polished it, restrung it and played it to get a feel for its sound. It had a very pleasing rich, mellow tone. Later, when I moved back to Australia, I found a musical instrument repairer in the Blue Mountains where I was living. He knew that maker as soon as he opened the case. It transpired that he also owned a mandolin made by the same man, one year earlier than mine! He showed me its special features that were Calace's signature. For example, there was a slipper of a different wood between the neck and the fretboard. It only cost me $50 for the repairs, and I know it would have been treated reverently and delicately by the restorer. I sold my other mandolin and that more than paid for the repairs to the Callace. Some years later, when trying to gather together enough funds to attend university, I sold the Callace to a girl who was very keen on Renaissance music, for the sum of $600. We both knew that she was getting a great bargain. 'Just give it a good home,' I said. I later sold my guitar, and eventually bought another mandolin — a beautiful, handmade one from Wildwood Instruments, Victoria, Australia. I think this is the best I have had of the six I have owned at different times. I later had to sell that one for food and a couple of utility bills when I couldn't raise the money any other way. I cried at having to part with it.

Church Bouncers

One Sunday Malcolm was going to preach at a church in East Osaka, an area that most Osaka Japanese have never visited and would be shocked to know exists. He asked if I would like to come and I shrugged and said, 'Sure'. I was always up for visiting places that I had not previously seen. He parked his car a few blocks away, and we covered the remaining distance on foot. I was horrified. Here were whole city blocks which had streets lined with people living in cardboard boxes and makeshift lean-tos. There were others in thick, unseasonal coats sitting on the footpath, begging. I saw a man peddling cardboard boxes from a flat-bed trolley, to which he had a dog and a cat tethered on frayed string. I had never seen anywhere like it and never suspected its existence. Surely wealthy Osaka could not possibly have an area so down and out, so grotty and impoverished?

Eventually, we reached the church, another shock: this church had solid steel doors and two large men acting as bouncers. All were welcome to the church but anyone drunk and disorderly was unceremoniously evicted. The pastor there welcomed us effusively. I sat in one of the rows of plastic chairs and Malcolm preached his sermon with the pastor acting as interpreter. Japanese from around the church's neighbourhood drifted in by twos and threes at the start of the service, killing time before the free meals offered by the church.

Afterwards, over a cup of tea and a meal in the church's basement, I had the opportunity to ask the pastor why there were so many people living rough in the area and he replied that it was an area that most people in Osaka preferred not to know existed. Most of the people living that way were company men who had lost their jobs and been unable to find new work in the dying days of the 'employed for life' economy. Others were estranged from their families for any one of a dozen reasons. He also explained that Japan did not have the same kind of social security system that Australia is blessed with. The security of lifetime jobs in Japan was now more of a myth than a reality. It was very sad and probably comparable to America's Skid Row. This was one more example of Japan's 'out of sight out of mind' credo. I returned home to Toyonaka with a much more accurate picture of life in Japan.

What Doctors Can Do

While I was living at Pension Yamaguchi, I was sitting Japanese-style one day and did a great deal of damage to my right knee when trying to stand. I had my first arthroscopy in a Japanese hospital and would not recommend it to anyone. Any surgery below the waist in Japan is routinely performed under an epidural anaesthetic rather than the general anaesthetic used in Australia for the same surgery. I had a room to myself, as Japanese are usually only placed in a single room when they are terminal, but they figured that a *gaijin* wouldn't mind. There was a thin mattress on the floor for my 'carer'. Meals were not supplied in many Japanese hospitals, and a friend or relative was required to stay with the patient for the first 24 hours following an epidural anaesthetic. Mrs Kitano from our church, kindly stepped in and acted as my guardian. After an epidural anaesthetic, the patient is not allowed to move their head for 24 hours. In Australia, there is no such restriction. Japanese nurses are not permitted to give injections or place drips, but what usually happens is that as soon as the doctor leaves the room, the nurse removes the drip and inserts it properly. A nurse whispered confidentially that sometimes the doctors completely miss the vein.

My pre-op tests involved two doctors and two nurses. The following conversation took place entirely in Japanese,

'Are you allergic to anything?'

'Yes. Morphine, rubber, adhesives, tea tree oil and people in white coats.'

The nurses tittered behind their hands but the doctors didn't even crack a smile.

'Oh, is that right?' Jab.

It really doesn't pay to joke with medical professionals armed with sharp objects as they may not have a sense of humour.

After the injection, the purpose of which I forgot to ask, assessing the time it took a patient to stop bleeding was apparently important. This interesting little ritual involved a scalpel, a stopwatch and a piece of blotting paper — which I eyed suspiciously. Various possible scenarios were ricocheting around the inside of my skull. Before I could arrive at a logical explanation, the scalpel blade was stabbed into my left earlobe, the blood was allowed to drip freely onto the blotting paper and the stopwatch was used to see how long it took for the blood to clot. Primitive, but effective. The Japanese firmly hold the belief that their physiology is fundamentally different from that of all other nationalities. I have had Japanese tell me that their intestines are longer than those of other nationalities. How they know this and why it would matter if it was true, I don't know. I found on dissecting a cockroach in high school, that the roaches have an intestine 18 centimetres long — I wonder if it makes a difference to them compared with those of other insects?

My leg was strapped and a special elastic brace was made for me, with hinged metal struts on either side so that with a movement of the hand I could make my leg straight or bent. Daisuke, the trainee Japanese pastor in our office, wheeled me and my crutches the one kilometre home each day with me perched on his bicycle but unable to ride it. I had to wear the brace for about four months, which made life a little awkward, especially given the Japanese enthusiasm for stairs as solution to differing building levels and squat toilets. I hopped the one kilometre back to the office over the railway line on crutches each morning taking more than an hour and leaving me exhausted by the time I arrived. I grew to appreciate how difficult life in Japan can be for anyone who is disabled.

I have a mild allergic reaction to some local anaesthetics. I assumed I would be given a general anaesthetic for the surgery, but Japanese hospitals use general anaesthetics as seldom as possible as there seems to be an inordinately high fatality rate of Japanese undergoing generals. So, I was given the epidural instead. I was lying on my back on the operating table, stark naked, wondering when they were going to knock me out. When the surgeon said to me in Japanese, 'Roll up like a prawn,' I began to panic. The fact that the surgeon administers the anaesthetic and not an anaesthetist sounded alarm bells for me and I was very worried about the type of anaesthetic they were going to use. After the injection I could see them waving a leg around; it looked like mine, but maybe it was someone else's. Being awake through the surgery was not a pleasant experience.

I learned a lot of new vocabulary from my experiences

with Japanese medical professionals and hospitals. Later, at university, I did my major essay in Japanese on 'Comparative Anaesthesia Practices in Australia and Japan and the Associated Risks'. My lecturer was really surprised and said, 'I didn't even know you knew words like this! I had to look a few of them up, myself.' I received a high distinction for my essay. It involved quite a lot of research, but it was worth it. My experiences in Japanese hospitals had certainly made an impression on me.

Living in Tennoji

After Malcolm and his family left Japan at the end of that year, I was seriously thinking of returning to Australia. However, Malcolm's successor was a Kiwi named Graeme Fawcett. Graeme asked me if I would stay on and oversee their office which was moving to Tennoji, in another part of Osaka. I said yes, and we found a flat for me about twenty-five minutes' cycle or ten minutes away by *chikatetsu*. Graeme was a different boss from the start; he was as concerned for our spiritual and physical welfare as much as for those of his flock. He was also keen for the auxiliary staff such as myself to learn as much Japanese language and culture as possible.

The church used to meet at a hotel in one of their function rooms every Sunday, followed by dinner together at a cheap and cheerful Chinese restaurant nearby, all invited. Another Kiwi named Paul and I often led the singing, but then we created a regular group with a pianist, two guitarists, a flautist, a violinist and me as mandolinist or guitarist if one of our guitarists was away. One of our tasks was to learn new songs, many of which were translated from English to Japanese or written from scratch in Japanese, and teach them to the congregation. I have never overcome my nerves when singing in public, but it was great to play with other musicians again and to be involved in the teaching and translation.

Graeme and his wife Lucy were two of the few people I have ever met who lived what they preached. Graeme's command of the Japanese language was formidable and was such that he did not need an interpreter when preaching. I think that it was partly because of this that his flock took him to heart more than they might have otherwise. When someone makes that much effort, you can't help but respect them.

Graeme stretched me by giving me tasks I had never dreamed I could do. As well as the administration work, I handled the phone and most of Graeme's correspondence. I also cleaned the office. We also began a ministry where I would go to the home of anyone in need of home help, and do whatever they needed free of charge, as well as teaching six English classes a week — three children's classes, a group of doctors, a housewives' class and a group of bank employees. That part kept me very busy. The home help idea didn't last long as we were hard-pressed to find local Japanese who would let us know that either they or a neighbour were in need of some help.

Lost Pup, Lost Child

One wet night as I was cycling home to Tennoji, Osaka, where I now lived, I had to brake suddenly as a small furry thing leapt out of the darkness in front of my bike. It was a tiny longhaired puppy, very dirty and scruffy. I put my bike on its stand, picked the puppy up and wondered what to do. I couldn't take it home as there was a strict 'No Pet' policy where I lived.

I knocked on a few doors and asked various shocked residents if they owned the pup; (I appreciated the fact that it's not every rainy night that you have a *gaijin* with a stray puppy knocking on your door). No one did. I then did the next best thing I could think of — I put the whimpering puppy in the basket on the front of my bicycle and took it to a police station I had passed in the previous block. I dismounted, gathered the puppy into my arms and pushed open the heavy glass door to see four Japanese policemen with their feet up on their desks, drinking tea. I explained what had happened and asked if they could take the puppy to an animal shelter, as I did not know of any and did not want the young puppy wandering around on the road in the rain, a fatality waiting to happen. They sagely concluded that, given its condition, the puppy was a *stetamono* — an abandoned stray.

Within minutes, one of the policemen had produced a little bowl of milk for the hungry pup, and two of them were kneeling on the bare floor playing with it. They could indeed take it to a shelter, but not until the next day, although this was something they had never been called on to do before, and was probably not in the police manual. Would I like some tea? They drew up another chair for me, and I chatted with them and drank my tea. They were intrigued by the fact that my father had been in various branches of the police force back in Australia — such as the Police Emergency Squad, the Stock Squad, the Drug Squad, the Mounted Police and the Criminal Investigation Bureau over a long career — and asked me lots of questions. We consulted a dictionary for some of the specialist words, but laughed and managed fairly well. The fact that I spoke Japanese made me something of a unique visitor, and they really seemed to be enjoying themselves, as was I. They were delightful, and it gave me a rare opportunity to ask questions about the different divisions and their roles in Japan. After an hour of furthering international relations, I said that I had better go home, and was invited to 'drop in again any time, any time at all'. Try that in Australia.

My only other (thankfully!) contact with police in Japan, occurred during my last three months in the country after the lease on my flat at Tennoji ended. I had moved that day to a homestay family who lived out near Osaka Bay, for my last three months in the country. One of my English classes was in Wakayama, an hour away, at a branch of the Sanwa bank, 6 pm on Tuesday nights, and my new homestay mother was in a fairly senior administrative position at the Sanwa Bank in the head office in Osaka's CBD. I had been teaching the class for several months already. I had only briefly met the family who would be my hosts, that morning, and went off to work as usual.

The heavens opened that night in a deluge and I discovered to my dismay that the subway station had something like six different exits. Unbeknown to me, I had exited from the wrong one and begun walking in the wrong direction. Without the family's phone number, I couldn't call the family to ask which exit I should take, I couldn't find the homestay, so kept walking along a closed market street that I thought I recognised from earlier in the day, but nothing really looked familiar. All had their steel roller doors in place for the night. Unless there was significant signage, it was difficult to determine at that time of day what kind of business each was. Unlike Australia where most of the wares were on display inside, in Japan, the wares are displayed outside the shop to entice buyers, and only returned to the inside at the close of the business day. After about an hour on a walk that should have taken me no more than twenty minutes, I found a small police station. I stood in their foyer, dripping like an exotic but badly designed water feature. I asked if they had a map of the area. Once they were over the shock of having a soggy, Japanese-speaking foreigner at the desk, two of the four asked me where I was going, and beckoned me over to a scale area map on the back wall of their office.

I produced the address of the homestay family, written

in Kanji in my dog-eared and damp notebook. They shook their heads and told me that I was way off course, about three kilometres in the wrong direction, in fact. I memorised the correct route, thanked them and turned to go. One of them insisted that since it was a fair way, was dark and raining, they would drive me home. I thanked them very much and declined, but they thought I was just being Japanese by declining. They insisted again and I relented, as I was incredibly tired and stressed by this time.

My initial thought was that one of them would just have brought the car around, would tell his mates that he would be back soon, and would drop me home. No such luck. The other policemen jumped to their feet and decided that it was such a difficult and important mission (not to mention a chance to break up a boring evening) that it would require all four of them to accomplish properly. They locked the glass front door, and put up a sign advising that the station was temporarily unattended. Two policemen sat in the front seat, with me in the middle of the back seat, flanked by two more of Osaka's finest.

With lights flashing — but thank God, no siren — we arrived at the right address about ten minutes later. Policeman Number Two in the front passenger seat stepped out of the car and rang the bell. Mrs Yamamoto came to the door and her hands flew to her mouth in horror at seeing a patrol car and police at her doorstep.

'We have a lost child for you, Mrs Yamamoto,' he smirked, jerking his thumb in my direction and reading the surname in *kanji* beside the house door. Policemen Numbers Three and

Four both opened their doors to let me out. Cringing and red-faced, I mumbled my thanks and apologies and bowed to all concerned. This was a humiliating experience of high degree on my lifetime scale of humiliations and defeats. The four policemen left with huge grins on their faces.

By the time I arrived at my bank class the following night, all of my students knew about the incident, joked with me and wanted to know what it was like to ride in a police car. Ah well, we *gaijin* have all the fun!

There Are No Kangaroos in Austria

There was a coffee shop called *Kikuichidoo* near Toyonaka station, where I used to go sometimes on my day off, to sit in a corner and do my correspondence. The coffee was bottomless, I had my own corner table which the staff 'reserved' for my use and they were all about my age and very friendly once they discovered I spoke the language. One of the waiters collected stamps, so I used to save all of my international stamps for him, which he said his grandmother soaked off the paper for him. As it was heated in winter and air-conditioned in summer, the coffee shop became my home away from home as my room had neither. Some days I drank so much coffee that I had stomach cramps and the shakes. I was the only *gaijin* who went there and they treated me like royalty. I became *their gaijin*. Some of the staff lived locally and we would smile, bow and greet one another in the street. When I lived there, I had the strongest sense of belonging than at anywhere else I lived in Japan. It was so nice to be recognised 'as one of the neighbours' instead of 'that *gaijin* who lives two streets over'.

I was amazed to receive quite a few of my sent letters returned in the post. Letters I had sent to people in Australia, on the front of which I had written the katakana for 'Australia', only to find that they had come back to me as undeliverable ... via Austria. My elderly postman used to become very agitated if he had to actually speak with me, as he spoke no English and was afraid of perceived difficulties involved in speaking to a *gaijin*. Even though I spoke to him in Japanese, he was convinced I was speaking in English to him and was sure he couldn't understand me. I explained further, with a deadpan face, that there are no kangaroos in Austria, and at last he understood the difference between 'Australia' and 'Austria'. A pity others in the Japanese postal system did not.

After that, most of my mail went through to Australia, and I continued to write the katakana for Australia on the front of the envelopes. My postman would smile at me and say good morning once we had the Australia/Austria difference sorted.

Reverse Culture Shock

Returning to Brisbane for a ten-week furlough in early 1987 was quite traumatic and bewildering. During those few short, blurred weeks; my maternal grandmother died from cancer, I attended her funeral, my father remarried, to someone I didn't even know he was seeing, I had surgery on my deteriorating right knee and caught up with as many friends as was humanly possible. Every day was spoken for. I felt disoriented, tired and having to clamp down hard on my uncharacteristically short temper.

Needing some extra money while I was home, the only thing I could find was to take in ironing at the rate of $3 per basket. With my gammy knees, it was hell and a lousy pay for something that I hate with a passion, no matter what the circumstances and no matter whose clothes they were. There are no ironable clothes in my wardrobe now, and I have figured out how to hang wet clothes so that any creases they may incur are smoothed out as they dry.

I returned to Japan unprepared and uncertain that I was doing the right thing. I had seen my future as working in Japan, and began to consider going to Bible College in Australia, then returning to Japan on a permanent basis. I never made it that far.

I experienced very little culture shock in Japan because I had studied the language and the customs for eleven years. What I did experience, what no one had told me could happen, is what is now recognised as 'Reverse Culture Shock'; also variously referred to as 'Re-entry Syndrome', 'Re-entry Shock', 'Cultural Cringe' and 'Own Culture Shock'. Reverse Culture Shock has now been widely noted as being experienced not only by missionary workers, but also by aid workers, released prisoners, soldiers returning home from overseas assignments, workers on oil rigs, and even in long distance truck drivers. People with Re-entry Syndrome experience some elation at returning home, but this is tempered or overshadowed by feelings of isolation, disorientation, loss and bereavement. It seems to have elements of Post-Traumatic Stress Disorder (PTSD). These people can be affected by the lack of some immediate goal which may translate as boredom or uncertainty. It is bewildering to be told repeatedly to 'pull yourself together and get on with it' when you have no idea why you are feeling this way, or to even recognise your own feelings. I have been able to help a few other people suffering the same thing I did, and see the light spark in their eyes as they suddenly understand what is affecting them, that it has a name and that a great many people suffer from it.

I found it very difficult to re-adjust to life in Australia and it has taken what seems to me to be an unreasonable number of years to do so. We humans take comfort from the immutability of the small things in life. The many changes that had occurred during my absence put me on the back foot mostly because they were unexpected. Even small things like coins were different, while I'd been away, one and two dollar notes were replaced by coins.

The morning I arrived back in Brisbane I went for a walk down Queen Street Mall, probably with my mouth agape, staring at all the funny-looking people. There were blondes, brunettes, people with black hair, tall, short, thin and fat. I was so used to a homogenous population, almost uniformly dressed in black or navy, that it took my mind some time to process what I was seeing. The best way I can describe it would be the impact of being too close to the brightly coloured explosions of a fireworks display, when one can be overwhelmed by sensory input.

It was almost two weeks before I transitioned to thinking in English again. It sounds very strange, but the reality was that I had become what is called 'a third culture' person — someone who no longer really fits in either their native or adopted culture. I had been told by my pastor that when someone goes away it is like pulling a fist out of a bucket of water — there is no space left behind and life flows into the space which was previously occupied by the person leaving for an extended time. Everyone gets on with the business of daily living, and it gives credence to the old adage, 'out of sight, out of mind'. I was determined to stay close in the hearts and minds of my friends and family and kept up a regular correspondence and was particularly grateful to those of my correspondents who would enclose newspaper clippings with their letters. This kept me abreast of current events in my home city to some degree, and helped lessen the full impact of Reverse Culture Shock.

I do not know how far Reverse Culture Shock has been researched to date, but there is certainly much more information available about, but not necessarily for, sufferers, their friends, families and colleagues than when I needed it. It may be coincidental, but I heard from a minister that there was a high (around 70%) apostasy rate amongst returned missionaries, partly because of Reverse Culture Shock and partly attributable to other factors such as a feeling of abandonment by God and their colleagues, friends and families.

Bible College, Katoomba

I began as a student at Commonwealth Bible College in Katoomba in February 1988, after a total of five years in Japan. The College was housed in two ex-tourist hotels, one on either side of the main road, a short walk from the famous Three Sisters rock formation along the cliffs. I was able to work part-time at the College as cook for students and staff, which helped pay my fees. My personal faith was surprisingly at an all-time low, and I think I was trying to force myself to believe things that in reality I no longer did. Nevertheless, I found my time at the College to be challenging, and stimulating. Some of the lecturers were genuinely inspiring. It only served to set up endless arguments of mental dialogue, however, for which I struggled to find answers. As a returning 'missionary' I was too embarrassed to go to anyone for help with what I was feeling. None of us knew that I was still suffering the effects of Reverse Culture Shock.

I experienced a low-grade continued abdominal pain which I had first known in Japan over the previous few years. I had had a couple of laparoscopies which had found nothing. I was told by several doctors that because they couldn't find any significant pathology, the pain must all be in my mind.

I was even sent to a psychologist, who simply put me on a prescription of medication for depression and sent me on my way. I *was* exhibiting the signs of depression, but that was an effect and not a cause. At one point, I was doubled over in pain across the door to a kitchen cupboard, and my supervisor at the College called the ambulance. I was taken to the Blue Mountains Hospital in Katoomba, where I underwent yet another laparoscopy and a D & C, which again found nothing conclusive.

A couple of my lecturers and some of the other students had been telling me that since there was no physical diagnosis, I must have sin in my life for which God was punishing me. I was beginning to believe it myself and underwent a lot of soul-searching to try to determine if they were right. What I read in the Bible was contradictory — on one hand there was the story of Job whose love and loyalty God tested through physical trials, certain that he would rise to the challenge. On the other were the stories of the New Testament in which God simultaneously forgave and healed individuals, and others where he only forgave/forgave and healed when they repented (of sin in their lives). I began to feel resentment and anger towards a God who could be vindictive and perverse, and misleading me into thinking I was meant to go to Bible College and meant to return to Japan as a missionary. By June, I was too sick to continue at the College, withdrew my application for the following semesters and returned to Brisbane.

In spite of my sometimes ill-health there, I could not resist playing the odd practical joke at the College. My first one was to swap the teabags in the lecturers' canister on their morning tea table for green tea bags — I simply swapped the tags over from the Bushells tea bags, then sat back to watch the fun. The college secretary was the first to notice that her tea was a peculiar shade of green when she poured in the hot water. Others followed. There was a bit of pandemonium before they realised that they had had a joke played on them. All fingers pointed at me during the ensuing general laughter. Another favourite students' joke was to Blutac the tongue of the lunch bell to the inside of the bell so that it couldn't ring. The bell was always on the lecturers' table and was rung as the signal to stand and say grace.

My jokes became more inventive as I went. There was a staff toilet in the hallway outside the main lecture theatre. I pulled the gizmo out of one of those musical greeting cards, studied it and figured out how I could use it. With a short length of cotton thread, a cardboard 'trigger' and some Blutac, I was all set. I went into the toilet, stuck the gizmo to the back of the toilet bowl out of sight, inserted the trigger to which was attached the strand of cotton. The trigger would be released when the toilet lid was lifted. I then attached the other end of the cotton to the lid, and made a hasty retreat.

Not long afterwards, one of our lecturers entered the toilet. A few of us stood around in the corridor to watch the fun. Suddenly we could hear the tune 'Congratulations' playing loud and clear through the toilet door. The beauty of the prank was that the occupant couldn't find where the music was coming from and had no way of shutting it off. Soon one of the male staff members emerged red in the face and a bit confused, which delighted the rest of us. Some of the students resorted to humming or whistling the tune whenever that lecturer walked past. Harmless, but fun. It gave me something else to think about and meant that I had less time to worry about my health, my sin status, and my studies.

My third and infinitely more sophisticated prank came during a double period of the subject God and Angels. Everyone loved the lecturer we had for that subject — David Parker. He had a great sense of humour and made the subject matter come alive. The auditorium was full — 150 people. The night before that particular double lecture, I enlisted one of the biggest guys in the class, who had a deep, booming voice. I set up a cassette recorder, left the first ten minutes of the tape blank and then recorded him yelling and banging, 'Let me out! Let me out of here!' I then went into the lecture theatre and duct-taped a little cassette recorder which had a speaker, up underneath the lectern with the speaker face down. The next day, after the first break in the lecture, I went out to the podium as though to ask Pastor David a question, which was our custom. While I was there, I surreptitiously slipped my finger beneath the lectern, turned the recorder on and went back to my seat. Ten minutes later, as he was hitting his stride with the second part of the lecture, there was an enormous racket, with yelling and banging, 'to be let out of here'. He looked under the lectern, saw nothing, looked behind him and out the door. Then said, 'Ok, who did it?' He was grinning the whole time. The laughing students all pointed in my direction and he wrote on the blackboard: Jessie 1, David 0. To this day, I think that was one of my most creative pranks.

Still, what goes around comes around. My room in the dormitory was directly across from the sewing room. Both doors opened inwards. All my fellow pranksters had to do was tie the two door handles together and I was a prisoner. I had to call out for quite a while before someone let me out and I was over an hour late for my morning lecture. I thought it was beautiful in both simplicity and ingenuity.

How to Find a Job

By August I was back in Brisbane, looking for work, and still suffering from the mystery pain and discomfort. One afternoon walking down Queen Street in the centre of Brisbane, I saw a sign in both English and Japanese that said 'Southern Cross Times Japanese Language Newspaper'. On a whim, I climbed the two flights of narrow wooden stairs, found the right door and gently knocked. It was opened by a tall Pakistani man and I was then sure I was in the wrong place. I asked if he knew where the Southern Cross Times office was located — I could see past him that there were just three dilapidated metal desks and two computers. He told me that yes, I was in the right place. Mr Khan invited me in for a cup of tea and a chat, and as soon as he found out I spoke and read the language, he offered me a job, starting the next day! I asked if he wanted to see my resume, but he replied offhandedly, 'Later, later'.

Bemused, I fronted up the next morning armed with my resumé, and a lot of questions as to what my duties would be. He had a Japanese girl named Etsuko working for him as well. As it transpired, my boss Mr Khan spoke no Japanese whatsoever! A strange job choice for someone with none of the language. He was, however, a smooth talker and managed to convince a lot of companies to advertise in his newspaper. The paper was aimed at incoming Japanese tourists as well as Japanese living in Brisbane and the Gold Coast, and carried articles and advertising in both languages.

Between the two of us, Etsuko and I managed the fees for advertisers, the advertising formats, the articles and translation of some, the overall design, the petty cash, office amenities and every other aspect of the newspaper except the actual printing and distribution, which were handled by a company in Ipswich. The position was only for three months but I learned so much in that time! I used my first computer there — an old Wordstar with green writing on a small black screen and perforated printing paper that used to escape and spill out of the box of its own accord.

When my three months were up, Mr Khan took me to visit a friend of his, Carmel, the Director of Key International College. She was apparently looking for a temp for three days to help with photocopying, collating and the like. I felt at home right away and she said on the second day, 'You know, I think we'll keep you.' So from a three-day temp job, I stayed three years, and advanced from general factotum to receptionist, to Carmel's Personal Assistant.

My miscellaneous tasks also included the photography for the College's domestic and overseas marketing materials, making use of my creativity, and being interpreter for students and other parties. For example, one fourteen-year-old female student with whom we and her homestay family had had no end of difficulty, managed to get pregnant and end up on drugs. The situation involved the police; her father had to be notified to come and fetch his daughter and take her back to Japan as she was expelled from the College. I suspect she had been more than a handful for her parents and that they had sent her to Australia in the hope that her behaviour would improve over here — out of sight, out of mind.

Because I had completed Intermediate and Advanced photography courses at TAFE, and as I did so much of the College's photography, one of my co-workers, Irinna, found a competition that she thought I should enter. It was being run jointly by Kodak and Verbatim. The two stipulations were that the photo entry had to contain one of Verbatim's five-inch floppy disks, and it had to be funny. I gave it some thought and said to myself, 'Why not?'

I used one of the disks, and a packet of plasticine, pipe-cleaners, a magazine and some googly eyes. I created a mouth around the hole in the middle, glued on the eyes, made pipe-cleaner arms and legs, and created little gloves and boots complete with laces and ribbed socks from the plasticine. I cut out pictures of people from the magazine and had them popping from the computer disk box, with the disk reaching in to pull one out, a backward slant on a person pulling a disk from a box. I sent it off and thought no more about it, until I had a phone call one morning at work saying that I had won the unanimous first prize. It doesn't sound like there was much serious competition. The person who won second prize merely had lots of the disks popping up from between the cushions on a lounge. Nevertheless, a representative from Kodak and one from Verbatim's Australian offices arranged a visit to the College to make me a presentation of the prize. All of the teachers released their students from class to watch and clap for me. Unfortunately, the prize was a video camera (I had rather hoped it would be still camera equipment). I used it a couple of times, then sold it. Part of the prize was to have my entry made into a poster for the coming year's advertising by Verbatim.

We had students from Japan, Korea, Indonesia, Afghanistan, Thailand, Hong Kong, China, France, Germany and Switzerland. I hadn't known that Korean men could grow so large until one morning, a disgruntled young Korean tried to barge into the Director's office because he wanted a refund. The fact that he had done very little study towards his course and seldom presented for class, didn't figure in his mind. I stood in the doorway with my arms braced on either side of the doorjamb, trying to stop him, but he just planted a hand on my chest and pushed me backwards. As far as security at the College went, I was it and I had just failed. I quickly called for a couple of the male teachers to come and help. He was given an interview with the Director and his class teacher and both agreed that he was not entitled to a refund, but that if he didn't start taking his classes seriously, he would be expelled and sent home. That quietened him down somewhat and he left the room with his tail between his legs. Fear of his parents being informed of his unacceptable behaviour was a powerful deterrent.

Tiananmen Square student uprising had just occurred a couple of months before, and suddenly we were inundated by mainland Chinese students, many of whom were enrolling in English classes as a backdoor way of immigrating to Australia. Some would appear for their first class and then disappear into a Chinese enclave, never to be seen again. Some were not so smart, they would come for their first class, disappear, and then reappear on the scheduled final day of their course for their Certificate of Completion. I would keep them busy while someone called the Department of Immigration, who would send an officer to arrest the culprits. The frustrating thing was that they would let many of them go if there was insufficient evidence to detain them or if they were screaming, 'asylum, asylum'.

The Chinese students who did stay and who attended their classes were poor and tended to steal everything that was not nailed down. We lost spoons, toilet paper, washing up detergent and a cassette recorder, paper, books and other stationery that we knew of. No way of proving who the culprits were, of course. The College did not want to go to surveillance level.

I did hear of a case where someone had rented a two-bedroom house to four of our Chinese students. What was later found was that there were six more living in the ceiling! As a result, all ten of them were evicted. We tried to help as much as we could in such matters, but sometimes the Chinese students would say, 'Yes, yes, thank you.' Then they would turn around and do the opposite thing to what we had suggested. This was a reminder that 'yes' can simply mean, 'yes, I hear you'.

Using my artistic skills, I took innocent-looking photographs of each of the staff members, and used the head of each one to create A3 montages using their heads and caricature bodies related to their roles in the College, with a humorous twist. I labelled the two pages 'Rogues' Gallery' and pinned them to the noticeboard one morning. By lunchtime, the students were howling with laughter over them, but no one knew where they had come from. The teachers and other staff gradually drifted over to see what the students were laughing at. Rather than be cross, which was a possible reaction I anticipated, I was besieged by staff and students requesting copies. I had selected everybody's unique contributions to the College and what they did above and beyond their duties to make the College special. Everybody loved it.

David Jones Department Store

When I first returned to Brisbane from living in Japan, I needed a place to live that was affordable. Another woman I knew was also looking for a place at the time, and we found an ideal two-bedroom flat together at Highgate Hill in Brisbane's inner south. Sharon had a job which took her away from home for a month or more at a time, and basically just needed a place to crash when she was in Brisbane. I had the smaller room, but after we had painted the whole flat, and I had sanded, wallpapered and varnished the dining alcove, it looked pretty good and was an ideal fit for our needs. I wish someone had told me before I did it, that the dust from sanding would penetrate every nook and cranny without drop-sheets and plastic being laid down first! I was there for around seven years, with a succession of flatmates, some good and some not.

At this time, I was not working, but studying photography at TAFE college in South Brisbane. I went through intermediate and then on to advanced level. I had seen a beautifully crafted wood and brass half-hour glass at David Jones department store in the City Centre, and went to their office on the top floor to ask permission to photograph it for one of my assignments.

'How long have you been doing photography?' asked the Receptionist.

'About seven years, from when I lived in Japan,' I replied.

'Do you speak the language?'

'Yes, I do.'

'Hang on a minute.'

She went in to the HR Manager's office and I heard only muted conversation.

'Mr Adam, this is Jessie Keyssecker and she speaks Japanese.'

I was invited in to speak with him. I told him that I was looking for permission to photograph the half-hour glass.

'We are looking for a part-time Japanese speaker for the Information Desk. It would be Friday night, Saturday and Sunday. The vacancy came up this morning. Would you be free at the moment to take it on?'

'Well, yes, but I ...'

'Good. That's settled.'

'Don't you even want to see a resume or something? Or test my Japanese?'

'Just bring in your CV when you start on Friday afternoon. Wear black and white.'

I loved the job because unlike most of the other employees, I didn't have the pressure to sell hanging over my head. I quickly built up a reference book of where to find unusual items such as walking stick tips, and miniature garden statues of Michelangelo's David, whether they were items stocked by us or not. We had a lot of repeat business at the Information Desk because people knew that if we didn't know, we would find out for them. One of the other major tasks of the girls on the Information Desk was to wrap gifts purchased by customers in the store.

There were some weird and wonderful shapes to wrap as well as the usual box-shapes. I managed the Christmas gift-wrap bar for two Christmases, teaching eight young casual university students each time how to wrap the various shapes including odd ones like tubes of hand cream and hexagons of Turkish Delight. The most interesting things I was asked to wrap were a deckchair in the OPEN position (not possible without putting one's fingers through the unsupported paper!) and to make a shirt look like it wasn't a shirt (I rolled it and wrapped it like a bottle). Sometimes, old ladies especially, would purchase tiny boxes of chocolates with just two chocolates in each box, and would present maybe 15 of them to us on the gift wrap bar to be wrapped and ribboned individually.

Thus began my career of part-time Information chick at David Jones for the next three years. The other people who worked there were wonderful, and I made several friends. Mike, the pianist, right in front of my desk, used to play my favourites for me as well as requests from shoppers. Add that together with the large bowl of fresh flowers on my desk each week, and I was convinced I had the best position in the entire store. Had I been in a financial position to do so, I would have paid them to allow me to do that job!

David Jones was experiencing a high volume of Japanese customers during that period which is why they wanted a Japanese speaker on the desk. Every day was different, and I loved the fact that we never knew what was going to happen or who we were going to meet during our shifts. While working there, I even received a marriage proposal from a 57-year-old Japanese business owner. He was serious, too, and sent several registered letters to me care of the store once he returned to Japan! That brought down a great deal of teasing on my head.

I was also pressed into service on the first day of the big Annual Sale for each of the three years I was there. The year before my first one, so many people had rushed onto the up escalator that it had started to run backwards and a number of people had fallen off. My job was to stand at the bottom of the escalator with my arm out and just let a couple of people on at a time. I actively sought out tasks for other departments too, such as attaching price tags, and other work that could be done while I was sitting there, as I hated having nothing to do, and saw no reason the girls under me should be idle either. It also relieved some of the tedium for the girls on the make-up and perfume counters. One memorable time, the security men football-tackled a shoplifter right in front of my desk. I pumped my fist in the air and startled shoppers as I called out, 'Yay, another one bites the dust!'

When our long-term lift driver Leo passed away, we had a new girl start in our ancient lift. During her first few days, she didn't quite have the knack of stopping at the floors but usually ended up somewhere in between. I brought my old driving 'L' plate in and displayed it on the metal front wall of the lift. The regular customers thought it was hilarious, and it brought a few smiles to others, but Mr Adam the man who had hired me, tried to hide his smile as he asked me to take it down. Miriam did improve with time, but then just as she perfected her lift driving skills, someone else took over. David Jones was very big on tradition. After Miriam, the new lift driver took over — he was the son of our long-time lift driver, Leo.

Once I had a blind date who I had asked to meet me at the Information Desk at the end of my shift. I stupidly mentioned it to one of the security guards, and when my date arrived at my desk, my phone rang and it was the security officer asking, 'Is that him?' I replied brightly so as not to give anything away, 'Yes it is, sir, thank you for your call.' The blind date was a flop, but the next morning, the security guard came to my desk and handed me a security photograph of the two of us.

'Just a little memento,' he grinned. 'Remember, I am watching you.'

I soon realised that with the penalty rates paid for weekend and night work, I could, if I was careful, live on that small amount of money, with the government student allowance, as long as I had a flatmate to share rent and utilities with. Having this part-time job was one of the factors that gave me the courage to apply for university studies, as, no matter what my subjects, the David Jones shifts would surely dovetail perfectly with the study week.

University Days

I applied for and was miraculously accepted by Griffith University Nathan campus, to pursue my Japanese language studies. I undertook a degree designated as 'Modern Asian Studies', with a major Japanese language study component. The first year passed uneventfully, and I worked tirelessly on everything I was allotted as core subjects and attained mostly Distinctions and High Distinctions for my work. It took me a little while to feel comfortable with university-style writing, but I attacked it with gusto, and really enjoyed the academic life, at this later stage of my life, perhaps more than I may have done when I was younger. I had no idea whether this course would make it easier to obtain work, but didn't think too ardently on the subject.

In most of my classes, I was either the oldest or one of a very few mature-age students. My ability to concentrate and my life experience in general gave me a distinct advantage over those who were fresh high school graduates. I was more disciplined than most of the younger students, who loved partying. Some of them used to skip lectures because of hangovers, and would freely boast about it. At first, one or two of them used to ask to copy my lecture notes, but after a very short time, I decided not to play the game any longer, and kept mostly to myself. However, it did not preclude me from making acquaintances of some of the students, which was useful for group work.

On campus, students could buy tea or coffee for 40 cents, and a biscuit for about ten cents. I quickly found a spot where I could regularly sit and study for a couple of hours, and failing that, I could find a small corner in the student library which suited my needs, and so spent most of each weekday on campus.

Sometime in my first year in 1993, the Griffith University library displayed a computer with a new thing called the 'World Wide Web'. A large number of students and lecturers examined the display. Most of us thought that as computers were so expensive, the Internet was merely a fad that would not catch on. How wrong we were, and how far the World Wide Web and computer accessibility have come in the years since!

I graduated in 1998, having saved enough money to take ten of my friends to dinner at one of the South Bank cafés afterwards. It was a great way to celebrate becoming the first person in my immediate family to have studied at and graduated from university.

Japanese Plus

The university load was particularly heavy during the third year as I was studying Japanese and Korean languages and each language had contact hours of 15 hours each week, comprising five two-hour lectures and five one-hour tutorials. Each language also required as much language laboratory (structured listening to tapes and doing verbal language exercises) access as possible, as well as about two hours' study for each every night. I knew I was taking on a huge load when I opted to do a second language on top of Japanese but I think it was worth it. I did very well in both basic Korean and advanced Japanese. There was also a range of other subjects each year which were an integral part of my degree, such as Sociology and Modern History of East Asia. I had terrific lecturers for most of my subjects, which made learning a pleasure that I revelled in.

While in my second year at university, I interviewed for a newly-created job and was successful. The Queensland Japan Chamber of Commerce and Industry, and the Australia Japan Society — Queensland had both decided after many years operating with honorary secretaries, that they would try operating jointly with a paid secretary. As there had never been anyone in that position before, it was my job to design it from the ground up. I negotiated with them that I would work for the QJCCI and the AJSQ Monday to Thursday, go to university on Fridays, and work Friday night, Saturday and Sunday in my part-time position at David Jones department store until I finished my degree. I was only able to sustain that load for about three months, and then had to say goodbye to my much-loved Information Girl position at DJs out of sheer exhaustion. One of the unwritten rules for the staff on the Information Desk was that if we were going to leave, we were responsible for finding our replacement ourselves. With ready access to other Japanese-speaking students at Uni, I had no difficulty finding someone to replace me.

As my final subject was an elective, I decided to do an art subject just for me. There were only 16 students in the class and we had a fabulous teacher named Peter, himself a practising artist. Peter took us through introductions to all of the major art media, as well as colour theory, perspective, etc. I fell in love with pastels and it became the medium I work in almost exclusively. I had difficulty getting home from the classes as they were conducted on another campus. My mum and her partner Mel came to my rescue, and on the nights when I was unable to find a lift with another student, they kindly waited for me until 9 pm and drove me home from that campus. It was a wonderfully energising time for me, and I absolutely loved it. The fact that Peter had to actually turn out the lights to make us go home, was a mark of how much we enjoyed his classes. We even had a night with a female nude model, and another with a male nude. At the end of the semester, we held a student art exhibition for family and friends — my first exhibition.

I moved from Nathan to a lovely home in Birkdale belonging to friends who were going overseas and wanted someone to house-sit for them. It was to be for three months, but ended up being for a year. It was much further to commute for work and Uni, but I had no rent costs, so it balanced out in my favour. My cat Opal didn't think much of the place, and had to be an indoor cat as she had been in the duplex at Nathan (with so much wildlife in the bush behind the duplex, I didn't want her hunting, something she had proved exceedingly good at in the past).

The Cat Test

While I was still sharing the flat in Highgate Hill, the old lady who owned the flats had a pregnant white cat. When it had its kittens, she was bent on drowning them. This was her idea of 'contraception'. As lively youngsters, the four assorted kittens would sneak up our two wonky wooden stairs at the back of our flat and have a great old time skidding around on the lino floor. I would shoo them out but one white kitten with amazing particoloured blue and yellow eyes was very stubborn and kept coming back in. I kept Opal as my cat, and we had 16 great years together.

After a couple of years Sharon moved back to New Zealand and I needed a new flatmate. I advertised in a couple of local churches, hoping for someone who had the same basic attitudes I held and who was unlikely to hold wild parties. Helen, a nursing student from Queensland University of Technology called to express her interest, and came by later with her then-boyfriend to look the place (and me) over. Helen was keen and moved in shortly afterwards.

Helen's boyfriend at the time hated cats. Opal made a beeline for him and rubbed herself all over him. Whenever he came around to visit Helen, he would leave with a liberal coating of white fur on his black trousers. We girls thought it was very funny. I mentioned it to the vet and she said that cats will head straight for the one person in the room who won't make eye contact, and that it was a domination tactic.

Helen and I were flatmates for about two years, and we are still very good friends, many years, a wedding and two children later (hers, not mine!). I had the privilege of being one of her bridesmaids when she married Mark in Sydney.

Because she worked shift work whilst attending university, Helen often needed to sleep during the day. At the time, a block of flats was being built next door. We had to lodge several complaints to the owners about the work starting earlier that they could legally do. Nevertheless, when our schedules allowed it, we had a lot of fun together.

One day I bought a big, boxy armchair from a thrift shop, but had failed to think about how I would get it home. Helen answered my cry for help and we managed to get it partially into her little hatchback Colt. We had no way of tying it into the back of the car, so I knelt on the back seat and simply hung onto the chair on the trip back to our flat. We made it to the back of the flats and then had to negotiate it up the back steps and into the lounge room. Horrors, we managed to wedge it firmly in the doorway at the back of the flat. Re-assessing our tactics, we decided to try the front door. This time we were able to eventually manoeuvre the unwieldy chair in through the front door without further difficulty. I still had that chair twenty years later.

Helen and I sometimes went to the movies together, and saw what was to become one of our favourites, the Australian film, 'Hercules Returns'. It was the most irreverent, politically incorrect movie either of us had ever seen. We left the cinema laughing and had tears rolling down our cheeks and quoted parts of the dialogue to each other all the way home, which would set us off laughing again. A year or so later, we decided to borrow a copy of the film to watch at home. Helen had two banana lounges which she set up in front of the television, I made a huge bowl of popcorn, and we 'went to the movies' and enjoyed the film almost as much second time around. There is no doubt in my mind, that were it filmed today, it would never make it past the censors. There was a Kylie Minogue joke in the film, and twenty years later she is still going strong and the joke is still current!

At that time, I was making novelty cakes for both money and pleasure. When Helen's birthday rolled around, I created a unique cake for her. It was a pair of bare buttocks with the trousers pulled down, crossed Band-Aids on one cheek and an icing hypodermic needle in the other. When she saw it, she held her sides laughing and said that all she had seen that day were bare butts! Her Mum thought it was in poor taste, but we thought it was great.

One cake that I made for a commission was a large, crouching pink pig with a mortarboard, rolled up scroll in its mouth, and a very happy grin on its face. It was for a party for a graduating policeman. When the woman who had commissioned it came to collect it, she nearly fell down the stairs laughing and thought it was even better than she could have imagined from my sketches. Another I made for my mum's birthday one year was a woman in a bathtub complete with frilly cap and reading a book. I had some problems with the icing, as it kept draining out through the bottom of the cake, just like water down the plughole. After a few minutes of trying to figure the problem out, I was able to plug the leak and make another batch of thicker icing. Mum had the dubious distinction of occasionally falling asleep in the bath and dropping her book in. She thought the cake was great.

I then progressed to my most ambitious cake yet: a grand piano with the lid open, all the keys correct and all the strings inside correct because I had visited a music store, and physically counted and diagrammed the keyboard of one. The store staff asked me several times what I was doing, and when I told them, they retreated, very puzzled. They had never had anyone do that before. Owing to the fact that they had no piano brochures, that and photographing a keyboard were all I could think to do. I confess that making novelty cakes is a lot of fun, especially when creating something original, and with no one to tell you it can't be done.

Helen moved on in the course of her studies, but we kept in touch and are still close friends. I then took in a Japanese student from a language college in the city, Rei. Having her there improved my Japanese and her English. I played tour guide and took Rei to all the local sights. Rei was lovely, and is still a good friend more than 20 years later.

Our block of flats was owned by an elderly Sicilian lady who lived on site and used to go through our garbage and wash our windows with a hose — sometimes when they were open! At one point, I bought a water bed and had a man come to install it. He connected the hose in the garden to the bed and began to fill it. Suddenly, there was a loud banging on the half-glass front door,

'You steala my water! You steala my water!' I opened the door and confronted her.

'You bad woman — very rude. I call the police.'

'No polizia, no polizia.'

The next day I saw her in the garden with her son talking animatedly and gesturing in our general direction. The only English I heard was 'Mama, you can't do that.' A little later, the old lady came to our door and said she was sorry.

'Okay. Next time I call the polizia.'

'No polizia, no polizia! You ... want ... more water?' she asked. Rei and I thought the whole incident was screamingly funny. The poor guy who was installing the water bed had no idea what was going on. He had that 'bunny in the headlights' look about him.

Rei was a delight from the start; keen to learn and see everything. I played tour guide and we took day trips together around Brisbane so that she could see more. She returned to Japan after a year, married and had a little boy. We still see each other on my infrequent trips to Japan and keep in touch through regular emails.

Whenever I interviewed potential flatmates, I liked to have the cat present. A couple of times I ignored the cat's responses and wound up with a very unpleasant flatmate — one Korean girl, one Japanese girl and one Irish-Canadian.

A male Korean student, Chung-Bin my next flatmate, was very agreeable. He was the baby of his family, with four older sisters. He had never had to lift a finger at home. I was surprised and pleased by his attitude — the first night he moved in, he pointed to the black wheelie bin behind the flat and said pointing to his chest, 'When? My job.' He was a guy who wanted to learn everything. He would say of almost every activity at home in the flat, 'Teach me.'

So I taught Chung-Bin to wash his clothes, hang them out properly, and iron them, how to vacuum, and how to water the garden without drowning it. We went through some simple recipes in the kitchen. After he had triumphantly baked a chocolate cake from my best recipe, he exclaimed, 'Take a photo please, *please* — my mother, she won't believe me.' So I documented Chung-Bin's domestic prowess, and he kept the photographs for his family.

Because I was always tinkering with things and making running repairs, he nicknamed me 'Miss Mac' after MacGyver, which was still a very popular TV series in Korea. He also told me that a pocketknife was called a MacGyver Kul (MacGyver knife) in Korean. Not something I could ever learn from a book. I rather liked the nickname and so was Miss Mac for the duration of his three month stay. For a guy who avowed that he hated cats, he and Opal got on very well, and she would often go to him for a cuddle.

I took Chung-Bin to task one day, as I knew for a fact that he had not written to his parents for almost two months. I suggested that we sit down together and both write to his parents. I laboured over my efforts, while Chung-Bin had no trouble dashing off seven pages. I asked him to correct my Korean, and we sent both letters off together. Actually, I had a bit of a nerve asking Chung-Bin to write to his parents, when

I hadn't written to my father since I left Japan. I had written to him monthly during my five years there.

Chang-Bin and one of his fellow Korean students were delighted that I was happy for them to cook Korean dishes in our flat. For some people, the overpowering smell of garlic is just too much, and Koreans *love* their garlic. They would also sit in the middle of the kitchen floor, with a clean garbage bag between them, mixing up a batch of *kimchi* by hand. *Kimchi* accompanies almost every Korean meal, morning, noon and night. It consists of Chinese cabbage, chilli, ginger and other ingredients, as there are many different variations. I love *kimchi*, as long as I don't have to kiss anyone or be kissed by anyone who has been eating it. Traditionally, it is layered in earthenware jars which are sunk into the earth up to the level of the lip, covered with a tight-fitting lid, and left to ferment. I love it fresh, too. Unfortunately, I only had the pleasure of Chung-Bin's company for three months before he moved on and he still remains one of the best flatmates I ever had.

My next flatmate, Soo-Yeoun the Korean girl student, hated cats, although she had said she was okay with them. She slammed the door on Opal's tail one day and broke it so badly that I had to race my poor cat to the vet where part of it was amputated.

One afternoon, I rescued Soo-Yeoun's washing from the line just as it began to rain, opened the door to put them on her bed and saw two overflowing ashtrays and the room stank of cigarettes. She had agreed when she moved in that she would not smoke in the house. I refuse to have people smoking in my house and I got rid of her as quickly as I could after that discovery on the grounds that she had ignored my house rules.

I moved to the leafy suburb of Nathan, and had no flatmate there until I met Martha at Uni. She was Irish-Canadian, had a terrible cold, and had just had to move out of the flat she had shared with someone else because the lease was up. I felt sorry for her and said that she was welcome to the second bedroom in my flat so she moved in that night. The penalty of not doing the cat-check was that I ended up with a rather strange flatmate.

The cat very emphatically disliked Martha from the beginning. Opal's covered litter tray was in the bathroom, as we lacked a laundry and they both seemed to want the room at a time when the other was using it. One winter night I came home from a late meeting to find Martha in her dressing gown, huddled on the front steps with the outside light on. I was puzzled by why she would want to sit out in the cold.

'What are you doing out here? It's freezing!'

'Your f#*king cat locked me out,' she muttered through clenched teeth.

Apparently, she had gone downstairs to put some rubbish in the bin, and Opal had headbutted the door shut, effectively locking Martha out of the house. She swore, too, that the cat had sat grinning at her through the glass panel beside the door. I'm afraid I was no use at all, I laughed so hard that I was in serious danger of peeing my pants. Opal had gotten into the practice of butting doors several years earlier whenever she wanted to access another room. In the flat at Highgate

Hill, we had had no internal doors except the bathroom door and bedrooms. I think she had decided that a mere piece of wood should not be an impediment to her. I told my vet about the cat's behaviour and she laughed and said she believed that cats were quite capable of doing things like that.

Martha also had an anti-electrical gravitational pull of some kind — she managed to destroy everything electrical in the flat. There was the vacuum cleaner, the toaster, and the funniest of all (being partly Irish — I'm sure there is an Irish joke about answering the phone while ironing), she managed to place the hot iron on the cords of both the phone and the answering machine, shorting out all three at once. She never offered to pay for any of the replacements, and being a student too, it was a very expensive time for me.

QFCCI and AJSQ

I worked with the Queensland Japan Chamber of Commerce and Industry and the Australia Japan Society — Queensland for a period of five years, looking after all of their meetings, minutes, functions and newsletters. I organised filing systems, and created and maintained their extensive membership databases, something I had never done before. It was during this time that my knowledge of computer programs skyrocketed. The job was busy and varied, and I really enjoyed it. I met most of the Japanese and Australian members, and some of them are my friends even now. I was also a representative for both organisations, and sat on a number of external committees, such as one for the Consulate General of Japan, and Redcliffe City Council's inaugural Kite Fest committee.

Both organisations held monthly committee meetings, sub-committee meetings, and social or business functions. I was largely responsible for organising them, choosing venues, negotiating prices and extras such as lucky door prizes, and it was a very busy job. I was also responsible for answering queries from the general public, and sometimes needed to research the answers before getting back to them. The funniest thing I was asked by a member of the public was how to go about working in Japan as a clown!

One strange thing that happened was that a Japanese man appeared on the doorstep at work one day clutching my contact details that someone in Japan had given him and told him that I would help him out. It transpired that he was a heart specialist contracted to work for a period at the Prince Charles Hospital at Chermside. It appeared that he knew no one in Brisbane and needed help finding a house, furniture and schools for his three children aged three, six and nine who were still in Japan with his wife. They would join him once he was settled. I felt it was my duty to help him in any way I could and a lot of it was done out of hours. When someone in Japan recommends you, you have an obligation to comply. Failing to do so brings shame on the person who recommended you, and doubts about their credibility. Maybe I have become a bit Japanese and tried to see the situation from their perspective!

I found a house for him, not far from three separate schools his children would need to attend because of their ages. It was difficult because none of the children spoke any English and it was complicated trying to persuade school principals to accept them, but I pointed out the cultural and social benefits to manage it! Once his family had joined him and were settled in, they invited me to dinner. There was another Japanese heart surgeon present, and all conversation was in Japanese. Between main course and dessert, the other heart surgeon began passing round what I assumed were holiday snaps. Not so: they were photographs of human torsos with no organs in them, with everything piled on the outside of the chest. They were interesting, but both doctors suddenly stopped in shock and said, 'Oh we are so sorry, we forgot you are not a doctor!' The photos were fascinating nonetheless. Mrs Okamoto played mandolin very well, and so I even found a mandolin orchestra for her to join, which she loved. I had the privilege of attending one of the orchestra's concerts as the Okamotos' guest.

The QJCCI holds an awards breakfast every year which is supported by the Japanese Consulate and the Department of the Premier who are the patrons of both organisations. One memorable breakfast began with my arriving half an hour before all of the members and guests as was my habit. As the Premier's Department was involved, we were using three flags instead of the usual two: Australian, Queensland, and Japanese. Even though I had drawn a diagram of the order in which the flags were to be hung according to the strict flag protocols, the five-star hotel still managed to get it wrong. I had to find a staff member very quickly to bring in their cherry-picker and swap the flags around. Flag protocol is something that not many people understand or even know exists. However, for those in Government or international trade, it may easily cause offense if the flags are not in the correct order. Thankfully, I was able to rectify this and any other bungles before members, guests and patrons arrived, none the wiser. This kind of mistake is inexcusable for a five-star hotel.

One evening I was to present an award from the Australia Japan Society to one of the students at Mt Gravatt High

School. I was in the front row with other guests, and looked up at the Principal on stage — it was none other than Mr Shrubsole, my Grade 12 class teacher at Corinda State High School many years before. He saw me and recognised me immediately. It was great to be able to catch up with him after the presentations. He was my favourite teacher at school as he was not only my class teacher, but also my debating coach, and teacher in charge of the school magazine, with which I was also involved.

The hours in this job could be very long, and I tried to avoid having a breakfast function and an evening committee meeting on the same day, as it was, I was often working from early in the morning until 8 or 9 o'clock at night. I did love the job, but in the end, noises were made about having someone else take over organising the functions side of the job. I knew this proposed person did not have a good eye for detail, and could only imagine what would happen if he forgot to take extra nametags, scissors, tape, pins, membership lists, etc. to functions.

In the end, I jumped before I was pushed. I applied for the position of Executive Assistant at the Mater Private Hospital in South Brisbane and was successful. I was to be not only Executive Assistant to the Executive Director, but was also to support three other Directors, the Board, and was also asked to take minutes for the Urogynaecology Committee and the Pastoral Services Committees. Initially it was to be for a short time, but they were happy with my work and asked that I continue supporting the sub-committees. The previous secretary had had a very tenuous grasp of medical terminology and had recorded the name of one of the Committees as the 'Eurogynaecology Committee,' which caused both laughs and gasps of horror all round.

ALONG THE WAY

Last Hope

I was still experiencing increasingly more frequent bouts of abdominal pain. Eventually, my GP referred me to a Professor Khoo at the Royal Brisbane and Women's Hospital. When I first visited him, I told him, 'You are my last hope. If you can't help me, I am going outside to throw myself under a bus because I just can't cope any more with this continual pain.' It was pain that was not acute, but sharp enough to mean that I could only barely cope with it. He performed another laparoscopy (my sixth) and diagnosed a condition in which I was receiving too much blood to the abdomen and it wasn't escaping properly, thus causing the pain by pressing on nerves and blood vessels swelling. He felt that yes, he could help me.

He also found that my ovaries were polycystic and that I had large fibroids in the uterus, both of which previous investigations had failed to show. These two things together rendered me virtually sterile. The relief that there was something physically wrong with me was such that I felt an enormous weight lift from my shoulders! He said it was a notoriously difficult complaint to diagnose because of the lack of particular pathology, but that it was actually a more common problem than either doctors or women realised.

Many women went through being told there was nothing wrong with them and to stop wasting their doctors' time. I then faced the prospect of a complete hysterectomy.

After my admission to the Royal Brisbane and Women's Hospital, Professor Khoo asked my permission for a couple of students to come into the room during his exam. 'Bring them all in,' I said "Make sure they learn, and don't put other women through the hell I've been through!'

The hysterectomy was straightforward, and I now had a 'grin' from hip to hip — uterus and both ovaries removed. Afterwards, I was ecstatic that apart from post-operative pain, there was none of that horrible, dull/grabbing pain that I had suffered for so long. It was like a miracle, and I couldn't wait to tell all my girlfriends to go out and have a hysterectomy, the best thing since sliced bread! While I was in hospital, many arrangements of flowers arrived for me, so many, that the nurses ended up placing some of them in the hallway, and, at my request, in the rooms of other patients who had none.

The flowers I received from the Consul-General of Japan really raised a few eyebrows, as did those from the President of the Australia Japan Society — Queensland, one of my bosses, Alex.

'Yeah, right, Alex. Nice joke,' I said in the hearing of one of the nurses, after reading the accompanying card.

'What's wrong?'

'Have a look for yourself.' I replied, disgusted, and passed her the card.

It read: 'Congratulations on the birth of your baby.'

The nurse left the room with a look of pinched

determination, but came back shortly after speaking with the florist in West End that had sent the flowers.

'I wouldn't be surprised if you receive some more flowers,' she said cryptically.

Sure enough, an hour later, a lovely bouquet arrived from the same florist. The courier poked his head around the corner into the room and asked breathlessly, 'Are you Jessie?' and at my affirmative but puzzled reply, he said 'Here, these are for you,' and dashed out again like a scalded cat. The nurse and I had some laughs at his expense.

Later, Alex, the AJS President and his partner Olwyn visited me in hospital. I wasn't going to tell him about the mix-up for fear of embarrassing him. However, I thought that with what I knew of his quirky sense of humour, he would gain some mileage from it after all. When I told him, he looked briefly horrified, and then gruffly said, 'Trust you, Jess, two for the price of one.' We all had a good laugh about that (I only laughed a little — I was still very sore), and it was at that point that I realised I was okay with the whole hysterectomy can't-have-kids-now aspect of the entire experience. At thirty-five, and not in a relationship, I felt that it was a moot point anyway and resolved to put it behind me, savour the good points and think no more of it.

My mother asked on the trip home from the hospital if I was 'okay with it,' which was as close as we came to discussing it. The flip side of not being able to have kids was the life-enhancing fact that I would never have another three-weekly ten-day heavy bleed with wildly-swinging moods, and strong pain. My girlfriends are jealous, believe me.

In terms of quality of life, I was in an infinitely better position now that it was over. I consciously avoided entering into relationships from that point on, figuring erroneously that every male in my age range would still be wanting to have kids and that I was a bad bet. I gently but firmly brushed off any male interest in me for about the next eight years. By then, I was sure that I was now in the non-child-bearing age group. Any guy who wanted me for a girlfriend would know what he was getting from the outset and would not be in a position to change his mind and cause both of us unnecessary anguish. I also figured, more correctly, that by this point, most of the guys who might be interested in me would have married, had a family and put the desire for children in the 'Done' column of their 'Life' spreadsheet.

Nobody Chews An Oyster

After I had accepted the position at Mater Private Hospital, my colleague and friend, Mark Bulley, then Japanese Guest Relations Manager at the Brisbane Hilton Hotel, took me out to celebrate my new job at the Hilton's Oyster Bar for oysters and champagne. It is said that it was 'a brave man who first ate an oyster'. This was my first personal encounter with oysters: they are slimy, green-grey things but with a fresh taste sensation of being from the ocean. I probably wasn't paying enough attention, because I don't remember whether Mark chewed or merely swallowed. Had I been paying attention, I would then have gained an authoritative handle on oyster etiquette.

Not knowing whether to chew or just swallow, and too embarrassed to show my ignorance, I took a punt and did both. The taste of the fresh sea was tantalising but the texture, which I am guessing is what oyster connoisseurs like most, was disgusting to an uneducated palate like mine. I have heard them cheerfully described by oyster lovers as 'slicker than snot'!

Casanova, the great Venetian lover of the 18th century, who was better known for the notches on his bedpost than his sermons or anything else, is recorded to have said in his memoir that oysters are 'a spur to the spirits and to love'. He should know — he started every day with 50 for breakfast. That is 18,250 oysters a year, just for breakfast! In his memoir he also recorded that he had seduced 122 women (and four men). Oysters have long been considered to be an aphrodisiac, along with figs, chocolate, strawberries, champagne, honey, grapes, garlic (!), basil, avocadoes, asparagus, vanilla, and almonds — to name a few. As with all folklore, there is usually an element of truth in there somewhere. Oysters are deemed to resemble the vagina (don't panic, girls!) and slurping and sucking them together as a couple is thought to be sexy. Casanova's preferred serving method was:

I placed the shell on the edge of her lips and after a good deal of laughing, she sucked in the oyster, which she held between her lips. I instantly recovered it by placing my lips on hers.

They are high in zinc which men lose in large amounts with every ejaculation, and testosterone, the male hormone which increases the level of dopamine, the feel-good hormone, in the brain when it is feeling 'in love'. They also contain two rare amino acids which help with the production of testosterone in men and progesterone in women. For a great night in, you know what should be on the menu!

So, what is the proper way to eat raw oysters? I am mildly disturbed by the thought of people walking along a beach with an oyster shucking knife, taking them straight from rock to mouth, while they are still 'alive'. How do you know when an oyster is dead? Does it have a brain? Does it feel pain? Intrigued by these questions, I decided to undertake an informal poll of friends and relatives, regarding oysters and to ask the experts. A scientist at the Queensland Museum responded that no, oysters don't have brains as such, they have nerve bundles called ganglia which dictate how and what the oyster does, which may or may not be interpreted as a 'brain'. Further research showed that the oyster does, however, have a three-chambered heart which circulates clear blood, kidneys, an oesophagus, stomach, intestine and a mouth of sorts.

I asked a cross-section of about forty friends and family, and friends of friends, 'How do you eat oysters?' Responses I received ranged from, 'Yuk, I would never put one of those things near my mouth' from a vegetarian friend, to 'I don't know', to a haughty, 'One does not chew an oyster, but merely savours it on the way down', to 'At $35 a plate in a restaurant, why *wouldn't* you chew them?' from my brother's girlfriend. She also mentioned that she was the one who had to shuck the three dozen they had just bought as my brother was hopeless at it. Of the forty or so people I polled in person, by phone and by email, the general consensus, however, seems to be that you swallow them if raw (although some insisted that they chew raw oysters too) and chew them if cooked, disproving my theory that nobody chews an oyster. We frequently assume that other people do as we do. Misplaced assumptions can at times bring us undone. Worldwide consumption of food oysters in 2010 was just over four and a half million tons, so obviously a LOT of people like them or, a few people like a LOT of them!

Oysters can, however, exact a revenge that is peculiar to their species. They can cause two major kinds of illness:

PSP (Paralytic Shellfish Poisoning) which is toxic and can cause death; and ASP (Amnesiac Shellfish Poisoning) which destroys brain cells and can cause permanent memory loss. Still love the little buggers?

I guess that as with most foods, one either becomes an oyster lover, or does not. Class me with the I-don't-really-care-if-I-never-eat-another-one section of the population. Although I love cooked mussels and love both raw and cooked scallops, there is something about the sight of a raw oyster that I find to be a real turn-off — maybe it is the sliminess, maybe it is the colour — I really don't know. But if there is anything on the menu other than oysters, I'm your girl.

A Scare

It was while I was house-sitting at Birkdale that I felt a small lump behind my left ear one morning, about the size of a large pea. I was three days away from graduating from university, and although I thought it could possibly be something very bad, I vowed that I would not see a doctor until after the graduation ceremony. I felt that I had worked too hard for too long to let anyone snatch that away from me.

The day after my graduation, I duly went to see a local doctor recommended by the friends whose house I was looking after. He scolded me roundly for waiting, and had me to a surgeon within the hour which made my head spin and scared the daylights out of me, as he thought it was probably a tumour. The surgeon did a fine needle biopsy with ultrasound to pinpoint it. I was in the Princess Alexandra Hospital before I knew it, and had the tumour and the left parotid gland removed from behind my ear and down my neck. Luckily, it was benign, but still took another three operations before surgeons were able to resect all of the tumour from around the Great Auricular Nerve and it had the potential to cause me to go deaf in that ear. The pain in between the operations was quite intense, and it wasn't until after the fourth surgery, about ten months after the first, that I was pain-free. Having the Damocles sword of cancer dangling over me for that duration was probably more emotionally draining than anything else I had ever been through.

My mother and grandad have since been through lung cancer and prostate cancer diagnoses, so I have some inkling of what it is like receiving news like that from a doctor. My maternal grandmother also died of breast cancer and my father from lung cancer.

The Firemen and the Cat

My next flat was in an old Queenslander house. It was very old and where it may have once had verandahs, it was enclosed. I had the western half of it. The cat had to endure another move and because the house was on a major arterial route, had to once more be an indoor cat.

There was a window facing the street and the cat used to sit on the sill, watching the world go by. She seemed particularly intrigued by the goings on in the Fire Station which was directly opposite. She would watch the firemen come and go, washing the trucks down and tending to the hoses. A few times, when the mood struck me, I would bake some scones or a cake or biscuits and take them across the road to the fire station. The firemen used to say to me that they never knew when I was there, but they always knew the cat was there. She made quite a pretty picture: white cat on a white sill, with a white lacy curtain as her backdrop.

I wrote a *Haiku* about her:

> Alert on the sill
> Welcome committee of one
> Awaits my footsteps.

She learned from an early age that 'No!' meant 'No! You had better stop what you are doing!' She made me laugh until I almost fell off the bed one night. I was stretched out reading and she was ensconced on the quilt at the foot, grooming herself. The TV was on and someone on the program shouted, 'No!' The cat stopped in mid-lick, looked at me and then at the TV with a startled 'What-have-I-done-now?' look.

Being a white cat, she was prone to becoming quite dirty, and so from the time she was a kitten, she had to endure occasional baths. She used to meow miserably from the bath tub but never tried to escape. I could take my hands off her and turn around for the cat shampoo and she never moved. The part she hated the most, however, was the one attempt I made of blow drying her. I have the scars to prove it. We compromised: I would towel her down and she would go off and dry naturally. Towards the end of her sixteen-year-old life she developed several skin cancers from her days as an outdoor, avid sun lover. She had a number of operations to remove them, and the vet said she had a few more years in her. However, after the last operations to cut her ears back to her head, I could see her winding down. I went out one morning after she had uncharacteristically gone back to bed, and when I came home, she was gone. I disinfected all of her things including litter tray, brush, lead, and collar and donated them to the local vet to pass on to someone who couldn't afford them.

Help, I Speak Japanese!

I contracted viral meningitis when I moved back to Brisbane, and was placed in a hospital room with a very strange old lady who kept insisting that I was 'stealing her oxygen' because the curtains around my bed were drawn. In the room next door there was a Japanese lady with tetanus, and the bed of another patient who had died during the night. I overheard the nurses speaking in the hallway, saying that they could not understand what the Japanese patient in the next room was saying. I called out to a nurse, 'I speak Japanese — Get. Me. Out. Of. Here!' They thought about it, decided it would solve their problem and mine, and made the switch without any difficulty or objection. The poor Japanese lady was in a bad way, had in a central line and was tortured with lockjaw, a symptom of tetanus. Thankfully, with injections every ten years, tetanus is now rare in Australia.

I was able to interpret for her and for the nurses, and even stumbled out of bed a few times to replace the cool cloth on her forehead. As she became better she said she wanted to take me out for lunch as a thank you. She told me I had been a godsend as she didn't speak English and was genuinely terrified every time the nurses came in to do something to her. We met up about three weeks after we were both discharged and went to a Japanese restaurant for lunch. I asked her how she had come to get tetanus and she said she had been gardening and cut herself on a piece of rusty metal. Tetanus is almost unknown in Japan and also here, so it may have taken a while to diagnose the poor woman. I wished her well and with much bowing we went our separate ways.

Art For Everybody's Sake

Having been well and truly bitten by the art bug at university, by pastels particularly, I signed up for a local art class, around the corner from where I lived. Classes were run on Tuesday nights and Saturday mornings. The classes were small, about ten students at a time, and so I went onto a waiting list. A year later, a spot opened up and I continued attending classes until they closed down about six years later, producing paintings at the rate of approximately one a week; sometimes longer intervals. The framer was just five doors away from my place, so I had it made and they treated me like a regular, often commenting on my work, 'I love this one, you should do more in this style' or, 'You are really maturing as an artist.'

One Easter Saturday, my good friend Lynn and I went for a drive up to Mt Glorious, which is one of my very favourite places in South East Queensland. We stopped at the Tree Frog Gallery, and chatted with the owner/curator for quite a while. Then my friend piped up, 'Jessie is a pastel artist and she's really good.' I wished the floor had opened and swallowed me.

'Bring me some of your work to have a look at,' Jackie said.

A couple of weekends later, armed with a car boot full of

paintings, we returned to Jackie's gallery. She asked us to lay them all out on a huge split-log table. She went over each one with a discerning eye and then stood up straight and said 'I will take these eight of the eleven, on commission.' I was over the moon — I had never dreamed that any of my work was good enough for a gallery! Jackie sat us down and began to talk to us seriously about having an exhibition there. I had only met her once before — how did my work impress her so quickly? There was another friend of hers named Marie who made felt wall hangings, and she thought the two would go well together. I was so excited but so filled with disbelief that I couldn't sleep for several nights. I had sold several paintings, mostly to workmates and was still in a state of disbelief that people actually wanted to buy them.

The date for the Exhibition was set for Saturday, 11 November 2000. We had proper invitations printed and I sent or gave one to nearly everybody I had ever met. Jackie had avocado trees growing in the yard behind the gallery, so nibblies consisted of lots of guacamole and biscuits, cheeses, and chateau cardboard wine. I had suggested to many of my friends that since the Grand Opening was at 2 pm, that they plan a picnic and make a day of it, which many did.

I was astonished that we had over seventy people in attendance; a great many of them friends and workmates of mine. I was deeply touched by their support. My sister, who was living in the Gulf of Carpentaria couldn't attend but sent me a beautiful arrangement of flowers to the gallery as a congratulations-and-good-luck. I think Marie sold about three of her pieces and I sold a whopping seven paintings on that first day. I had to keep pinching myself. The exhibition ran for three weekends and I sold one more painting during that time. Since I had only supplied eight paintings in all, that was 100% sold. Wow. That fact required several hours, no, days to digest!

The only exhibition I had participated in until then was the student exhibition at the end of the semester of art I undertook at university. Since then, I have had two solo exhibitions in the Hamilton Library — sold one painting — to my mum, who wouldn't let me just give it to her. How's that for embarrassing? It was not a venue that encouraged people to want to buy the work, but more of a look at some local artists' work.

Working at Mater Private Hospital, South Brisbane, I sold another three large paintings and one commissioned work. I even sold a large painting (biggest one I had ever done — the Gateway Bridge over the Brisbane River in fog) to a girl I saw every morning on the bus. I let her pay it off as I do with many of my buyers, and it just makes it much easier for them and makes them more ready to commit to purchasing the painting. Half of the time I forget about it and am surprised when they come to me with money. Another couple from Redlands bought five of my paintings. I get a real buzz out of visiting their home and seeing my paintings throughout. One afternoon I had collected a newly-framed large work and had it held gently with my knees on the short bus trip home. It was a semi-abstract rendition of The Gateway Bridge in Brisbane, in fog. The colours were muted blues and greys. A young lady with whom I'd chatted several times previously, sat beside me and was in raptures about how much she liked the painting and how well it would work with her décor. I mentioned that it was for sale. We struck a bargain for a figure and knowing she was on a budget, I suggested she just give me some money as she could and pay it off like a layby. I didn't keep track but relied on her honesty. She loved the large painting then, and I hope she is loving it still.

When I was a Receptionist for Disability Services (Queensland Government), Pam, one of my workmates, had a strong connection with a small Indian orphanage, and decided to hold a book auction to raise funds. The idea was that staff would bring in books they no longer wanted and we would bundle them up in lots of four and people would bid on a bundle. I asked her if she would like some paintings, too, and she replied that yes, that would be great. I think she was expecting maybe one or two, but I brought in my largest suitcase full of fourteen small to medium sized paintings, left over from my exhibitions and not likely to sell. We displayed them in an empty pod in the office for about a week before the auction.

On the day of the auction, I thought a couple might sell, but my jaw must have hit the floor — all fourteen of them sold! With all the proceeds going to help the orphanage, we made over a thousand dollars, just from the staff of our small office! None of the paintings sold for their true worth, but that didn't matter — as long as they raised some money. Some staff bought them for gifts, some took them home and some put them up in their pods at work. Pam and I were both ecstatic.

Since I worked in a pod alone as the Receptionist and

needed quiet for the phones, I decided to put up four paintings in my pod and called it my mini-gallery. I wasn't looking for buyers, but various staff drifted in and out to have a look at what I had there. Three of the paintings sold, two to the same man. The two he bought were a portrait of four fearful Vietnamese kids I had done for myself and never had ambitions to sell, and the other was four leafless trees in snow on a pale blue background. He said it reminded him of Narnia. The title of that one was *One is One and All Alone*, as one tree was standing separately from the other three. I took the title from an old English folk song called *Green Grow the Rushes-O*, which had a first line of 'One is one and all alone and ever more shall be so'. When I began painting, my goal was to paint songs, and by extension, poetry. You know how a line of a song or poem will travel around and around inside your head ... known in the music industry as 'ear worms' because you can't get them out of your head and they become like a burrowing worm in your mind. Some powerful visual stimuli can do the same thing.

At one time when I was out of work, the two ladies who owned the Ascot Art Supplies which was connected to the small studio where I attended classes, asked if I would like to work in the shop casually. I jumped at the chance and worked hard to gain sales by being as helpful to customers as I could be. I also created special displays for Mother's Day and Easter. My Easter display was a white rabbit with a beret I had crocheted, painting at an easel, bearing the message, 'Happy Easter from the Easel Bunny'. It earned me a few funny comments. For Mother's Day, I decorated a blank canvas with chrysanthemums surrounding it and the words: A picture is worth a thousand words, paint Mum a picture this Mother's Day.

One of the two ladies worked in HR at the BP Refinery on Bulwer Island and through Kelly Girls Recruitment Agency, asked for me to be their receptionist for three months. I enjoyed it immensely, and from the front window, I could see hares, foxes, a wallaby, and an unbelievable variety of birds. Sometime after Karen had left the company, I had a call from Kelly's asking me to again take on the role. I explained that I would love to, but had no transport, as Karen used to pick me up and drop me home, as she passed by my door. The lady phoned me a half hour later and said that they were so keen to have me that they were prepared to pay my taxi fare each way, every day for three months! I have never felt more wanted in my life! Needless to say, I worked my hardest for them so they could justify such an unusual arrangement. This, too, was a job I really enjoyed and was sorry when the temporary position ended, and the incumbent returned from her extended leave.

When David was younger, he used to climb and abseil at the Kangaroo Point cliffs on the Brisbane River, opposite the Botanical Gardens. I wanted to paint something special for him, so painted the cliffs in a slightly abstract way, but I must have done something right as he was able to point out different sections and name the different climbs in my painting. My framer liked it and told me I was really starting to mature as an artist. David has it hanging on his office wall and I like to think that he thinks of me every time he looks at it. I presented the wrapped parcel to him, sitting together in the bow of one of Brisbane's city cat ferries, just as we glided through the shadow of the Story Bridge. As the Kangaroo Point cliffs loomed closer, I gave him permission to open my gift, so that he was looking down at my rendition of the cliffs, while the real thing loomed closer on our port side. He loved the painting, and thought the way I had chosen to give it to him was very romantic.

A couple of years later I painted him another, of Mt Lindesay at dusk, with a full moon rising. We'd been there together, but its major significance to him was that he and his father used to climb and camp there together. He can be endearingly nostalgic sometimes. That painting has joined my other, on the walls of his office.

I continue to paint but find it takes more to inspire me these days, and feel the need for a specialist pastel teacher now, rather than just a general art teacher. Still looking for one. Life took a very unexpected turn around that time, and out of necessity, I was forced to shelve my musical and artistic pursuits. To cut a long story short, I've had both knees replaced, loads of exploratory surgery, and have had a total of ten organs removed. As I pointed out to my doctor, it was the worst weight loss plan I had ever heard of! He laughed heartily and said firmly, 'Well, at least your sense of humour is intact. That's something no doctor has figured out how to transplant yet!'

The Break In

Living in the old Queenslander which had no alarms or security screens other than Opal's sensitive hearing. I was awoken at about 3am one morning. I heard a great thud on the tin roof of my flat. I guessed it must just be an overweight possum and was on the point of grumpily seeking sleep again. However, I suddenly felt it must be more than just a large possum and I was instantly awake. I strained to capture and analyse every tiny sound. To my absolute horror, I heard the sound of boots tramping slowly and very deliberately up my front stairs. The intruder grabbed the screen door and bent it, undid the catch and tried to break down the wooden front door. He damaged the strip of wood that protected the catch of the lock, but didn't make it any further.

Then I heard his heavy footsteps descend, tread heavily around the side of the house and up the back stairs where he tried unsuccessfully to break down the back door to gain access that way. By this time, I was huddled on the kitchen floor in my nightdress, on the phone to the police. I hope everyone who has been in this situation has had the same kind of help I had that night from them. The operator said the police were on their way and did I want her to stay on the line until they arrived. 'Yes, please,' I whispered.

Then I called out to the intruder, 'You'd better take off. My husband is calling the police!' I later thought that was pretty good thinking for someone who was still sleep-befuddled and single.

The police arrived within ten minutes — two cars and a dog unit. Apparently a man had tried to break into one of my neighbour's homes which housed two elderly ladies just fifteen minutes earlier, and the police made the fair assumption that it was probably the same man. After searching nearby backyards, they couldn't find him, even with the dog. The policeman and policewoman who interviewed me could obviously see that I was scared out of my wits. I must have looked like 'The Wreck of The Hesperus' as my dad had been fond of calling his girls, especially when we dared come to the breakfast table with hair uncombed and clothes askew. (Look it up — it was a real ship.) The two first responder police asked if I wanted them to stay with me for an hour or so, just to make sure he didn't come back. I thanked them profusely and accepted. I was sweating, shaking, and barely able to speak with shock. I was so impressed by their care, that I wrote a letter of thanks to their boss the very next day, commending both officers for their care beyond duty. Thankfully, the would-be thief and/or worse, did not return. The police were fairly certain it was someone after money and readily saleable items to fund a drug habit. Because of this episode, it was determined that I have a resultant case of Post-Traumatic Stress Disorder. Even now, I can seldom fall asleep before 3 am.

One afternoon soon after the attempted break in, I was chatting with the two old ladies who had coincidentally been broken into four times. It worried me that the old ladies were as lax as they were with their security. On many occasions I walked past their home to see the front security door and wooden front door either unlocked or wide open. One told me that the police had suggested to her that she keep a can of flyspray by the bed in case she was broken into again.

'The policeman said to hit them in the eyes with the fly spray and it can't be construed as a weapon,' Alice chuckled at the novelty of this idea.

I thought this was excellent advice and have taken it to heart. Look out future would-be robbers! Another piece of advice I was given was to have a large pair of men's boots by the front door, as the thief will think twice about breaking into a home where a large man lives. This, too, I have done and was lucky enough to catch a friend just as he was about to throw out his old size-13 work boots. A piece of protection of my own devising, which I plan to implement soon, is to have a full dog's water bowl by the door, inscribed 'Killer' and a heavy dog's leash draped over the trellis by the front door as further deterrents. By employing a few simple strategies, it is possible to completely rewire the would-be attacker's perceptions of my home, in turn altering his assumptions of who might live there, and bypass me in favour of an easier target.

At the time of writing this, three years have elapsed and my sleep has been fragmented and unrefreshing ever since. Not only do I have to contend with traffic on one of the busiest roads in Brisbane, but every little sound out of the ordinary startles me instantly wide awake, heart pounding. Many other women who live alone must go through the same thing, and I really empathise with them. I sleep with a large knife under my pillow and would not hesitate to use it should the need arise. The only problem is that I have cut my fingers on it a couple of times in my sleep and bled on the bed linen! Some nights I wake and have to go and check the locks on the doors. Maybe I have the beginnings of Obsessive Compulsive Disorder (OCD). However, the precautions do not seem so extravagant when I think back to the Papua New Guinea sailor who missed his merchant ship one night and begged to be allowed to sleep in my entry way. While sympathetic to his plight, I did not know him and there was no way I was going to let him sleep there. I directed him to the sailors' church and went back to bed. The incident rattled me because it could have been true, but then again it may have been a ruse. I wish I could have given him a warm place to sleep, a pillow and warm blanket, but the risk to my personal safety was simply too great.

Another Crossroad

I have been brought to yet another crossroad in my life. I am excited. I wonder where life will take me next? I have applied for over 180 jobs and have been told by employers that there are 300-450 applicants for each job … and over-fifties are not wanted, in the same way as convicted felons trying to return to the workforce. When did we 50-somethings, with a wealth of knowledge accrued over a lifetime, lengthy list of skills, and excellent work ethics, become so undesirable? Still, it is not all doom and gloom — I have had eight interviews. There is a change in the wind, time to move on. I surely have to crack it eventually. Once I ended an interview by placing a block of Cadbury's fruit and nut chocolate on the table and saying, 'This is not a bribe — it is a physical embodiment of some of my best qualities: I am sweet, a little nutty, can solve most problems and am not past my use-by date.' Hopefully this will make my interview stick in the minds of the interviewers and raise my profile above those of other job seekers. In the meantime, I have looked on these few months as a gift of time to write the book I always wanted to write.

I have given up trying to find work because of the physical and psychological ailments I have. Some will improve; others will not. I now live quietly in an over-55s unit complex, confident that I will see out my days here, with a sweet rescue cat. My life has been one of serendipity, simply sometimes being in the right place at the right time. It is not necessarily something that one can orchestrate. Certain circumstances can position us for the chance of a lifetime, or open the way for us to achieve further goals. Of course, there is a place for planning and formal study otherwise one may never achieve one's goals. I may never have become a governess had not Del moved into the flat opposite mine. I may never have worked at David Jones had not my photography lecturer set that particular assignment that brought me to their store. My friends think I am very laid back, but I try not to worry about small things, and tackle the hard stuff when it crosses my path.

Although I have long suffered from depression that can be so debilitating that I find myself turning into a shaking, crying mess, I fight it, and I fight it. Still, on some days it will unpredictably and inexplicably squeeze me so tightly that I am unable to get out of bed, breathe normally, eat, sleep or socialise on any level. Friends, even those who are initially very sympathetic, eventually reach a point where they just can't listen any more, even fearing that they too may be dragged down into the stinking morass. Others cannot be judged when they are ill-equipped to provide the help and support one needs, and 'fail' you. This is where a trained and sympathetic professional can be the best person to talk to. When you gaze into the box, the view is vastly different than seeing only the view from within those same four walls. One of the best pieces of advice I have ever received is:

IF YOU ARE GOING THROUGH HELL, KEEP GOING.

The world is your oyster chew carefully.

THE END

(of this bit, anyway)

If you have enjoyed this book, please feel free to post a review on goodreads.com, or contact me on my personal email: sjessiek@gmail.com

Book Club Questions

1. What did you like best about this book?
2. What did you like least about this book?
3. What other biographies did this book remind you of?
4. If you were making a movie of this book, who would you cast?
5. Share a favourite quote from this book.
6. Would you read a novel by this author?
7. What feelings did this book evoke for you?
8. What songs does this book remind you of?
9. If you had the chance to ask the author one question, what would it be?
10. Does the book succeed in bringing the people and places to life?

www.ingramcontent.com/pod-product-compliance
Lightning Source LLC
Chambersburg PA
CBHW021138080526
44588CB00008B/114